Handmade Type Workshop

Tips, Tools & Techniques for Creating Custom Typography

Acknowledgments

I'd like to thank all the designers who gave over time to submit
work for this book as well as create work specifically for it,
particularly those who created the tutorials. Without your help
and contributions this book would not have been possible.
Thank you also to the team at RotoVision for their continued
editorial support. This book is for Mum and for Daniel.

HANDMADE TYPE WORKSHOP.

For more excellent books and resources for designers, visit www.howdesign.com.

15 14 13 12 11   5 4 3 2 1

Distributed in Canada by Fraser Direct
100 Armstrong Avenue
Georgetown, Ontario, Canada L7G 5S4
Tel: (905) 877-4411

Library of Congress Cataloging-in-Publication Data

ISBN 13: 978-1-4403-1037-9
ISBN 10: 1-4403-1037-8

Art direction: Tony Seddon
Cover design: Lisa Båtsvik-Miller and Sarah Lawrence
Design concept: Lisa Båtsvik-Miller
Design and layout: Fineline Studios

Handmade Type Workshop

Tips, Tools & Techniques for Creating Custom Typography

Charlotte Rivers

Contents

Character creation

Font creation

Introduction

◄ *Window display, Mathilde Nivet, Paris, France*
ORIGAMI JEWELLERY
Hand-cut 3D letters.

The creation of lettering and type is an inspiring and experimental area of graphic design, not to mention versatile. Lettering and type are complex disciplines that are constantly engendering innovation and reinvention. Type is everywhere, guiding, teaching, and speaking to us. It is an essential starting point for creative communication.

With the arrival of computers, specifically the Mac in the 1980s, the designing of fonts became a largely digital affair, but recent years have seen a return to the popularity of the art of the handcrafted letter. Along with many other areas of design, the aesthetic of the handmade type is a rapidly growing trend among designers, illustrators, and type enthusiasts of all stripes. That is not to say that computers are no longer involved, as typically they are, at some stage in the process. However, they tend merely to serve as a tool for design.

Traditionally seen as the purview of professional typographers, lettering is now created freely and without boundaries by all manner of creatives, and the number of different methods and media that are being used to create it is seemingly infinite. From hand-drawing with pencil and paper to knitting, sewing, and stitching, to using light installations, jelly, and even toothpaste, designers are communicating messages in many different ways. Such experimentation simply proves that one of the things that makes lettering and type so fascinating is the flexibility to interpret, and sometimes even break, the traditional rules of creating it.

Shown throughout this book are examples of type design that will inspire, energize, and fuel creativity. The book also provides practical details on how to go about creating different type and lettering. The first section explores different ways in which lettering and type can be created and includes chapters on the hand-drawn, printed and stitched, digitally drawn, 3D or installation-based type, and found and photographed type. The second section outlines how to take handmade type and create a complete working font from it.

Together these examples demonstrate that the ways in which to approach a brief that requires words or letters goes far beyond what is available on a designer's Mac or can be bought online. From creating illustrated to installation-based type or photographing found type, the solutions are many and varied. Of course not only is creating original lettering or type by hand an opportunity to make a unique font specific to a particular project, it is then also owned by its creator, forever.

▲ *Decoration, Mathilde Nivet, Paris, France*
N
Hand-cut floral display creating a letter in the negative space.

◄ *Illustration, Alina Günter, Zürich, Switzerland*
WITHOUT CUSTOMERS IF NECESSARY
Hand-drawn in ink on paper.

Introduction

Character creation

Chapter 1:
Illustrated or hand-drawn

Hand-drawn lettering and type have become more and more popular in recent years, with many designers often choosing this avenue as a solution to a design brief. It provides designers or typographers with the opportunity to express their creativity and to add their own personality to a design project. The ways in which designers work to create their hand-drawn type are many and varied; for example, working in pen, ink, pencil, Sharpie, watercolor, the list goes on. Some designers work to create extremely intricate hand-drawn letters using a highly considered structure; for instance, Dutch designer Hansje van Halem's Doily type on pages 14–15. Others create their work in a more free sense, developing the letterings' shape and style as they go; for instance, Lisa Congdon's Swirl type on pages 18–19. Either way the examples of hand-drawn lettering and type found on the following pages are always highly expressive and, of course, unique.

PROFILE Hansje van Halem

Amsterdam, the Netherlands

Hansje van Halem works mainly for print (books, brochures, and invitations) and exhibition signage. Clients include the Dutch Post, for whom she designed a series of stamps. She has a gallery in her home called Schrank8, which is, in fact, a 1930s showcase cabinet housed in her living room. Every two months van Halem invites a graphic designer to fill the cabinet with their work. Openings are held and there is an associated blog. In addition to this, in her spare time van Halem draws letters, which may become a complete typeface. She finds inspiration in all sorts of things, including paper, secondhand books, the view from a plane flying over a mountain, books about textiles and handcrafts, a pencil drawing of a leek, the bubbles in Coca Cola, sausage wrapping paper from Switzerland, office supplies, the computer, systems, repetition, and the challenge of endurance.

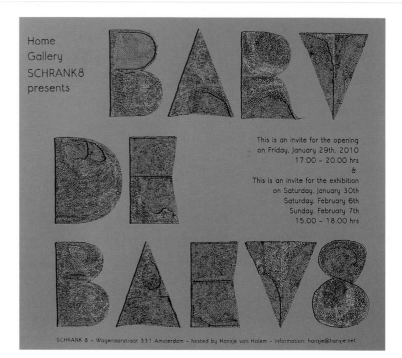

▲ *Exhibition invitation*
HOME GALLERY SCHRANK8 PRESENTS BART DE BAETS
As the name suggests, van Halem created the Marker Dot type using a marker pen.

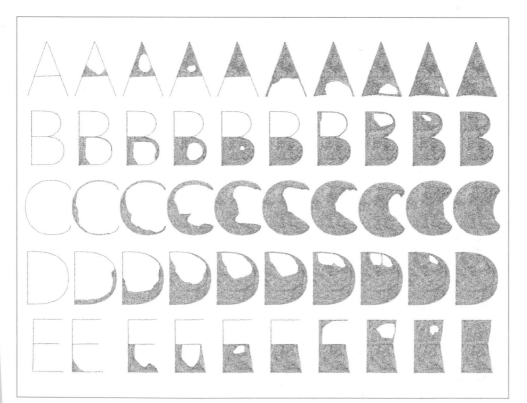

◄ *Marker Dot development* **Various letters**
You can see how the letter develops from a simple line drawing into intricate work.

"For years I've only been making letters drawing directly into Illustrator, perceiving it as digital hand work," explains van Halem. "But I got bored with the limitations of drawing on the computer and started to draw with a fine liner on paper. I find it enormously liberating, but do still miss the sharpness of lines in Illustrator." She adds, "I love graphic design because I love reproduction... The best thing about drawing letters and making alphabets is that they are yours. For me it means that they are exclusive."

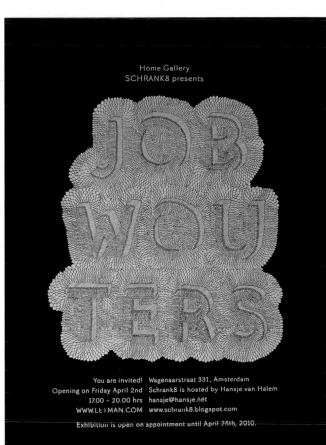

▲ *Exhibition invitation*
JOB WOUTERS
Van Halem's Hook type was all that was needed by way of graphics on this exhibition poster.

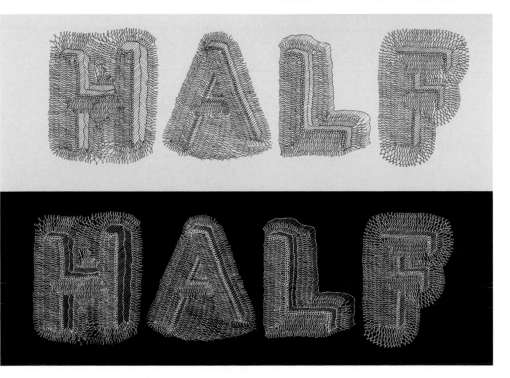

◄ *Illustration*
HALF HALF
Hook type created using a fine liner.

◄ MATHIEU,
ALEXANDRA,
DAVID, KATELYN,
ROSANNA, JON

Hansje van Halem's Doily type was originally created for a poster announcing the 30th birthday of the W139 Gallery in Amsterdam. The type was inspired by a book about Brussels lace. "I didn't try to copy it and in my enthusiasm to start working, I didn't even investigate the craft," she explains.

"Instead, I picked up a 0.3mm fine liner and started to draw shapes around a letter skeleton on paper. My aim was to make a lot of different versions to avoid using the same letter twice." Today the collection of letters is still growing.

INGREDIENTS

- Pencil
- Fine liners
- Eraser

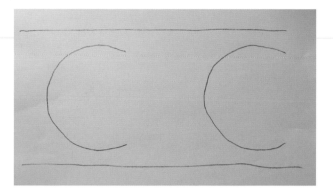

Step 1

Draw two lines that will form rulers to guide your letter height and then create a letter skeleton with a pencil.

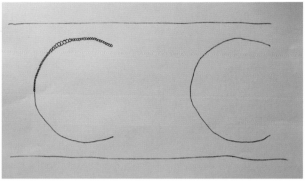

Step 2

For this step you need to use a fine liner, to differentiate from the penciled letter.

Step 3

Choose a pattern you like—circles, intertwining lines, geometric shapes, or anything that inspires you. Then draw the pattern around the letterform outline. Keep your first pattern drawing quite small. Erase the pencil skeleton, leaving the skeleton drawn by the fine liner.

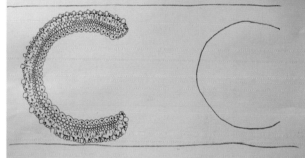

Step 4

Begin to add to the letter, growing the pattern as large as you wish.

Step 5

Once you've drawn your first letter and are happy with it, go on to draw different letters. Don't be afraid to vary the design with each letter, depending on the shape. Some letters lend themselves to different sorts of pattern, e.g., the ascenders and descenders in letters like P and K. Use the counterspace in letters like O to enhance your design.

PROFILE Lisa Congdon
San Francisco, USA

What started as an interest and hobby for San Francisco–based artist and illustrator Lisa Congdon has now become her livelihood. Congdon has been making things with her hands since she was very young. She is completely self-taught and works primarily by hand, using gouache, pencil, and ink. However, she does step into the digital by scanning and manipulating hand-drawn elements on her Mac. Congdon also likes to experiment with different printing techniques, such as Gocco printing and screen-printing. As a commercial illustrator, Congdon's inspiration for her work comes from vintage typography, nature, and color, and this very much shows in her style of illustration and typography. "I very much enjoy designing and creating type," she explains. "There are just some things that we can convey in art and design, using the written word that we cannot convey through pictures… For me, making the written word look beautiful, by creating a beautiful typeface and incorporating it into my art, is very satisfying. I sketch all of my typefaces for several days until I get what I like using a rollerball pen and my Moleskine notebook." Congdon creates work for a variety of different clients, including independent publisher Chronicle Books, fashion and lifestyle store Urban Outfitters, and paper goods company Madison Park Greetings. She also co-owns Rare Device, a design-led, San Francisco–based store and art gallery, with designer and curator Rena Tom.

▲ *Type sample*
Alphabet
When designing this font, Congdon wanted to create something that was decidedly hand-drawn, as opposed to a refined digital typeface.

A B C D E F G H I J K L M
N O P Q R S T U V W X Y Z
a b c d e f g h i j k l m n o p q r s t u v w x y z

▲▼► Type sample and illustrations
Alphabet / BLOOM
Congdon created this font for inclusion
in her own art and printmaking practice.
It was created over a number of days using
a rollerball pen and a Moleskine notebook.

◄ Logo
NOISY DOG STUDIO: MODERN PET ART +
PHOTOGRAPHY
The client requested a logo and hand-drawn type
that was bold and also casual. "I love hand-drawn
type that mixes upper and lowercase lettering
in different ways," explains Congdon.

▼ Illustration
Alphabet
This font was created
for Noisy Dog Studios,
a pet-potraiture
company in the Pacific
Northwest of the USA.

ABCDEFGHIJKLM
NOPQRSTUVWXYZ

TUTORIAL Lisa Congdon

San Francisco, USA

◄ IT'S ALWAYS WORTH IT.

INGREDIENTS

- Pencil
- Black liquid ink
- Fine-tipped brush
- Black ink pen
- Eraser

Another font created for use in her own art and print-making practice. The idea behind the design was to create a type that combined traditional block letters with wild swirling elements. Congdon created the type using pen and ink in her Moleskine notebook. It usually takes her a few attempts over a few days to develop an idea and create a typeface that she is completely happy with, before drawing the final version.

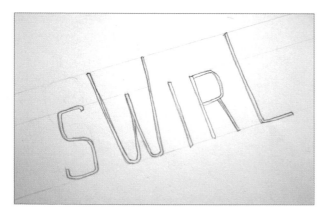

Step 1

Using the pencil, lightly draw straight lines that will guide the height of your letters. Then, also in pencil, draw the basic forms of the letters.

Step 2

Still using pencil, add "swirls" on as many of the letters as you like. This is free form and there is no right or wrong way to make them.

Step 3

With ink and brush, ink in the basic letters. Work on only the basic lettering first. You will add the swirls in ink (or fine-tipped pen) later.

Step 4

Allow the ink to dry completely, so as to avoid any smudging.

Step 5

With a fine-tipped pen (or continue with the ink and brush if you are experienced), ink in the swirls, adding in more width to the lines at various points and leaving them finer at others.

Step 6

Allow the piece to dry and then erase any remaining pencil marks.

Step 7

If you have started with one word, you can then go on to create a complete Swirl alphabet.

PROFILE Natsuki Otani

Tokyo, Japan / London, UK

Otani is Tokyo born and raised but for the last few years has lived in England. "This experience has really helped and given me a much more open, more diverse outlook. In addition to this, I've also gained a wealth of visual tools I never imagined possible," Otani explains. Otani works mainly using ink on paper and loves to include vibrant and bold colors within her work. Inspired mainly by music, she creates her type freehand, often drawing "from her heart" and finding inspiration in the everyday and in what is around her. "Being a designer is all about giving people a nice life experience, which is something that makes me proud when I feel like I have succeeded with a brief or made people smile," she explains. "I like creating and using typefaces, as they give a strong and direct form of communication; they use language directly, as opposed to illustration, which uses images to get its message across." Although Otani is just starting out in her career, she has already worked on a number of different commissions, including work for magazines and musicians.

▲ *Illustration*
I'M SO HAPPY TODAY
This type was created to, as Otani explains, "make someone smile for a moment."

Illustration Rally

THURSDAY, 8 JULY 2010

Flickr

This is a test post from , a fancy photo sharing thing.

POSTED BY ILLUSTRATION RALLY AT 09:23   0 COMMENTS

SUNDAY, 4 JULY 2010

Belarus - A difficult past.

ABOUT THIS BLOG

ILLUSTRATION RALLY

Illustration Rally is a massive international rolling collaboration which takes a theme and runs with it! copyright© All images on the blog are copyright of each artist. Please do not copy or reproduce without explicit permission of the author.

VIEW MY COMPLETE PROFILE

LABELS

Alphabet (26)
Hand drawn illustration (16)
European Countries (6)
Collage (3)
Mixed media (1)

▲ *Blog masthead*
ILLUSTRATION RALLY
As the audience for this blog is the illustration community, Otani wanted to create a type that captures freedom, positivity, and ease.

▶ *Greeting card*
THIS MEDICINE WON'T HELP YOU.
This type was created using ink and watercolor on watercolor paper as a message for greeting cards.

TUTORIAL Natsuki Otani

Tokyo, Japan / London, UK

◄ *I! My! Me! Mine!*

This type was created by Otani using ink on watercolor paper. This is Otani's favored way of working and she creates much of her lettering in this way. Starting with a chosen type that has been manipulated, or an original hand-drawn type, she will play around with the letterform until she achieves her desired design. Once satisfied, Otani will begin to work on inking in each of the letterforms.

INGREDIENTS

- Sharp pencil
- Watercolor paper
- Brushes
- Inks
- Eraser

Step 1
Carefully draw an outline of the type on to the watercolor paper using a pencil.

Step 2
Using a brush, fill in the type with water. Make sure you stay within the penciled outline. This is to make sure that the ink will stay within the font.

Step 3
Drop ink into the water and let it soak into the paper. Do this directly from the ink bottle or use a brush; you get stronger colors if you use ink straight from the bottle.

Step 4
Draw the water through the font, adding inks as desired before it dries.

Step 5
Once finished, let the work dry out thoroughly.

Step 6
When it is dry, you can then carefully erase the pencil lines and your type is complete.

PROFILE Walrus & Eggman

Barcelona, Spain

Walrus & Eggman is a design studio run by Silvia Rojas and Iván Gómez. The duo tends to specialize in designing for the music industry, from CD and LP artwork to posters, with their main clients being Junior Mackenzie and Orthodox. They have been working together for a number of years now. "We take care of all of our works like little babies," they explain. "It doesn't matter if they are big or small projects, we always keep our passion like it was the first project we worked on."

◄ Logo
PLAY BY DIR
DiR is a chain of gyms in Barcelona. Walrus & Eggman created the logo using pencil on paper and then assembled it, together with the other elements, in Photoshop, Illustrator, and FreeHand.

▲ Poster
26 HAPPY BIRTHDAY PARTY, ENEL BABA CAFE
This personal project was created for Rojas' birthday. It was hand-drawn and then traced in FreeHand.

The duo begin all their projects drawing by hand, using pencil and paper, before turning to the computer to complete their work, using FreeHand, Illustrator, or Photoshop. Despite their use of computers, they are very much fans of the handcrafted. "More than creating typefaces, what we do is create hand-lettering and for us that makes it more personal, closer, and different from the rest," they explain. "It keeps us going, keeps us inspired… We are inspired by so many things. Every day we check our favorite design blogs. We love going to flea markets and checking out things like old books and manuscripts, magazines, and so on. Then, of course, there is music. We can't stop listening to music, buying records, and going to gigs. I guess we design record covers because we are frustrated musicians."

▲ *Poster*
JUNIOR MACKENZIE & FRIENDS THAT SING,
"SONGS FROM THE TOP OF A MOUNTAIN"
This poster was created for an acoustic gig by band Junior Mackenzie. The design of the type was inspired by old wood-block type and was hand-drawn in Illustrator before having texture added to it in Photoshop.

▶ *Album cover*
JUNIOR MACKENZIE
Inspired by posters from the late 1960s, Walrus & Eggman created this album cover for the band Junior Mackenzie. The type was created by hand, using pencil and paper. The color was added in Photoshop.

TUTORIAL Walrus & Eggman

Barcelona, Spain

◀ Los Reactivos: Too much is never enough

INGREDIENTS

- Pot of nail polish
- Paper
- Scanner
- Adobe Photoshop
- Adobe FreeHand

When Walrus & Eggman were asked to create the album cover and packaging for the band Los Reactivos, the brief was to create something that represented the music—pop, punk. There was little time to create the artwork and, to this end, it was decided that creating a hand-drawn type was the best option. "We started doing sketches using pen or pencil but ended up using nail paint, which suited perfectly for what we had in mind," explain Rojas and Gómez. "After writing out the logo, album title, and song names, we scanned everything and assembled it in Photoshop. The layout was created using FreeHand."

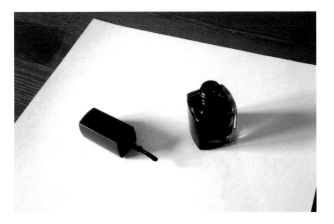

Step 1

Draw the required letters out by hand, using the brush that comes with the polish. Using this method is great for creating an interesting texture.

Step 2

As well as the required letters, you could also complete a whole alphabet, so as to make a complete font.

Step 3

Once all the letters have dried, scan them and then use Photoshop and FreeHand to arrange the type in any way you desire.

PROFILE Yoshi Tajima

Tokyo, Japan

Yoshi Tajima graduated from the American Intercontinental University in London with a BA in Communication Design and has since worked freelance under the studio name of Radio. He works with clients mainly from the music, advertising, and editorial industries, creating beautiful hand-drawn type, black-and-white illustrations, bold lettering, and logo design. Most of his work is created by hand using a pencil, although he does work in other media, such as collage. Inspired by Art Nouveau, much of his work features delicate, ephemeral imagery and elegant illustration. "I love drawing with fantasy in mind," he explains. "My illustration

◄ *Illustration* Alphabet, GIGOLO TYPE Created for Gigolo Records in Germany, the idea with this type was to create something dirty and aggressive that would appeal to the target audience: techno lovers. It uses many different images found in magazines and arranged like a collage into letters.

style is based on my own fantasies, which mainly consist of finding the right balance between confusion and order… I work a lot within the music industry, which I love, as designing and working on projects within such an industry brings with it the opportunity to explore new trends and inspirations—to be experimental."

▶ *Book cover*
PARIS CIRQUE PARIS
This type was created by Tajima for use on a book cover. He first hand-drew the letters using pencil on paper before finishing them off in Photoshop.

◀ *Illustration*
MAGIC
Tajima created this dark, mysterious type inspired by trees and their branches.

CHARACTER CREATION *Illustrated or Hand-Drawn*

TUTORIAL Yoshi Tajima
Tokyo, Japan

◀ FORM

Tajima created this type in homage to German biologist, Ernst Haeckel, and the idea that nature, which develops out of, and into, itself, is beautiful. Its letterforms can be created using any existing type, which is sketched out on paper and then embellished using a fine pen.

INGREDIENTS

- Pencil
- Paper
- Fine-tipped pen
- Eraser
- Scanner
- Adobe Photoshop

Step 1
Begin by drawing out a rough sketch of a chosen letterform and the type of embellishments you want to add, using a pencil on paper.

Step 2
Use a fine-tipped pen to draw over the pencil outline, using a dotted line technique. Once you have finished this, erase the pencil outline.

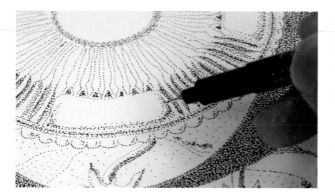

Step 3

Fill in the letterform, again using a dotting technique and a fine-tipped pen.

Step 4

When you have filled in the letterform, add shadow and emphasis to different parts of the letters by over-dotting the dots. Do not fill in the letterform with lines; use only dots.

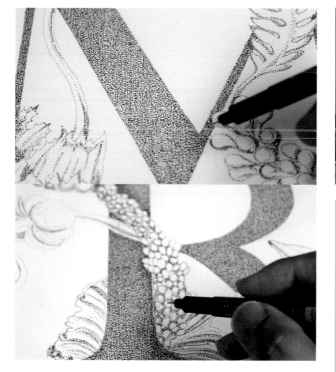

Step 6

Scan the letters and import them into Photoshop to add color to the background.

Step 5

Continue to do this with all your chosen letters, until you have completed them all.

CHARACTER CREATION *Illustrated or Hand-Drawn*

PROFILE Charlotte Lord

London, UK

Charlotte Lord graduated from the London College of Communication's typo/graphics design course and completed internships at Point Blank Collective and Black Dog Publishing before deciding to go freelance. She runs her own studio, specializing in typography and identity, web, and editorial design. Lord works for clients in the charity, environmental, and arts sectors. "I love working to a brief and enjoy the challenge and responsibility of communicating on someone else's behalf," explains Lord. "I am also inspired by the project itself: its opportunities and challenges, the client and the audience, the process and the end product." Lord works in whatever medium best suits a project; however, each idea always begins with hand-drawn sketches, particularly with her type design. "I have always been fascinated with letterforms and the way in which they can convey an idea or tone in such a myriad of ways, and how to apply these in beautiful and functional designs," she adds. "Typeface design is perfect for creating a unique 'voice' and is a challenge I particularly enjoy." Lord's design inspiration comes from Herbert Spencer, particularly his work on *Typographica* magazine and *The Penrose Annual*. She is also an avid collector of old printed ephemera, which she collects from bookstores, markets, and online auctions.

▼ ▶ *Leaving card*

BYE BYE CHRIS BOOT

This card was created for Bruno Ceschel, an editor who was leaving Chris Boot Publishing. Lord had been experimenting with modular and geometric shapes, and used this as the inspiration for the design by drawing out modular letters on graph paper. She then transposed the letters into 3D using isometric graph paper.

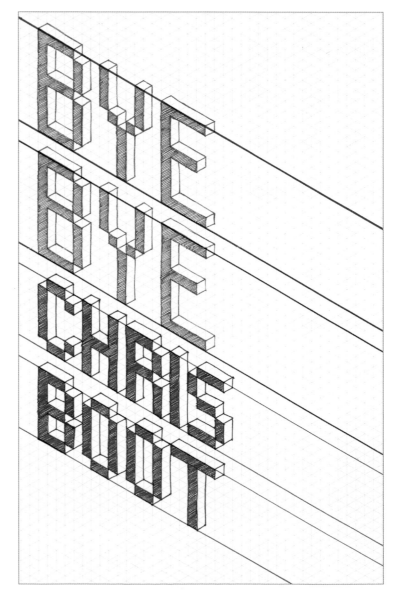

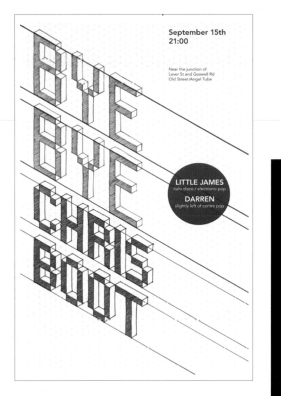

September 15th
21:00

Near the junction of
Lever St and Goswell Rd
Old Street/Angel Tube

LITTLE JAMES
italo disco / electronic pop
DARREN
slightly left of centre pop

◄ ▲ *Notes*
I'M SORRY, I DIDN'T
HEAR ANYTHING. / FOR
MORE INFORMATION,
PRESS THE STAR KEY.
Scripted Behaviour
features a hand-
drawn version of
the Monoco typeface
created by Lord using
pencil on paper.

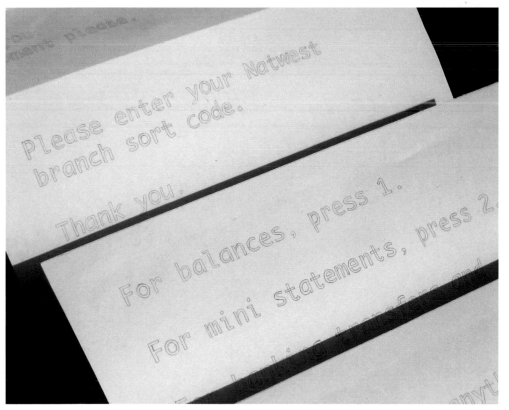

CHARACTER CREATION *Illustrated or Hand-Drawn*

◄ WE PLAY MUSIC

Lord was commissioned to design a logotype for London-based DJ and promoter duo We Play Music. "I wanted to create a logo to reflect their simple, playful name," she explains. "I took inspiration from children's building blocks and the geometric designs of Mondrian and the Bauhaus.

I wanted the logo to be very robust so that it could be used in any setting but also strongly relate to its fashionable East London audience." Lord began to create letterforms using only simple geometric shapes. These were then developed to create better legibility and stronger overall design.

INGREDIENTS

- Pencils
- Graph paper
- Craft mat

Step 1
Begin by sketching out geometric shapes. For instance, use two triangles to create the W and M and then semicircles for the curved letterforms.

Step 2
You can add shading to accentuate certain overlaps. This extra design element shows the construction of the letterforms.

Step 3
Once you have completed the letters you require you need to scan and import them into Adobe Illustrator and then draw the path of each shape separately.

Step 4
You can now experiment with different object fills and stroke widths.

Step 5
Refine the outline of all your letterforms. In this example, filling in the counterspace on the U helps to unify the logo. The outline of the P has been simplified and the balance of the shapes on the S improved.

PROFILE Sneaky Raccoon

London, UK

Anna Mullin works under the name of Sneaky Raccoon. As well as working on her own projects, she also works as a designer for Kidrobot creating vinyl toys. "I've always been interested in drawing, exploring creative ideas, and problem solving," she explains. "Despite completing a degree in fine art, I knew that my future lay in graphic design, so I set up Sneaky Raccoon while in my last year at university, which enabled me to work freelance on illustration projects while building up my portfolio and studying." Since then Mullin has worked on many different projects, including for Nike, Sawdust, Airside, the BBC, and *Print* magazine. "My process of creating work is pretty organic," she explains. "I often have a vision of what I would like the design to be before I begin, then draw and redraw for as long as it takes for a strong composition to be realized… I am inspired by all things around me, I am observant and like it when I see something unusual or something that makes me laugh," she adds. "I like to take photographs of interesting things I come across, as they are always a good source of inspiration."

▲ *Illustration*
MUSTACHIO
The aim of this hand-drawn lettering was to
create a typographic layout that was shaped
like a moustache.

◄ *Illustration*
AMERICAN CLASSICS
This lettering was created in collaboration with
Sawdust for *Nude* magazine. The idea was to
create a typographic headline based on iconic
American diners. It was hand-drawn and then
redrawn in vector format in Adobe Photoshop.

TUTORIAL Sneaky Raccoon

London, UK

INGREDIENTS

- Mechanical drawing pencil with a 0.5mm lead
- HB pencil
- Eraser
- Lightweight paper
- Ball of string
- Scanner
- Printer
- Adobe Photoshop

This was created for US design magazine *Print*. The brief was to create a design for a tote bag based on a charity of Mullin's choice. The concept of the resultant design is the old memory aid of tying a knot in order to remember something. "That concept is contradicted in the condition of Alzheimer's disease where memory is affected and often lost," explains Mullin. "Here, the string becomes the memory that you have already forgotten to tie, as well as symbolizing the journey of a life from beginning to end with its own path and twists and turns." Mullin began drawing a continuous line of type and continued to do so until the composition worked fluidly. She then enlarged the composition using a scanner, printed it, and then redrew it, which enabled her to create more detail within the drawing.

▲ FORGET ME NOT

Step 1

Begin drawing and redrawing different compositions until you are happy with one. Sometimes, a little serendipity actually changes the direction of the composition. Here Mullin was attempting to make the string into a forget-me-not flower shape, which was in the end discarded in favor of a more circular shape.

Step 2

Scan and enlarge the composition, then trace the drawing onto another sheet of paper to make a simple guide that will be visible through the lightweight paper used in step 4.

Step 3

Next, take the ball of string and use it to experiment with how the lettering would naturally flow within the composition, if it were composed using string. It is useful to understand visually how string unravels and bends.

Step 5

Fill in the segments of each thread to make the string appear more three-dimensional and twisted. Once completed, scan the drawing, import into Adobe Photoshop, and adjust the levels to enhance the contrast of the lines.

Step 4

Place the guide you created in step 2 under a sheet of lightweight paper and begin drawing the string in more detail, one line at a time. Refer to your actual piece of string as you draw tricky twists and bends.

GALLERY

YOU'LL EITHER LOVE THEM OR YOU'LL HATE THEM

◄ *Advert, Al Murphy, New York, USA*
YOU'LL EITHER LOVE THEM OR YOU'LL HATE THEM
This comic-style font was created for use in a Marmite ad. It was drawn by hand before being scanned and cleaned up in Photoshop and finally Illustrator.

► *Illustration, Katja Hartung at Toben, Sydney, Australia*
LIFE IS LIKE AN ONION
This self-initiated piece was created as a T-shirt design submission for the Live Cancer Foundation. Hartung hand-drew the lettering emerging from the onion using pen and paper. This was then scanned, cleaned up, and overlaid on a simple circular spot of color.

▲ *Painting, Chris Rubino, New York, USA*
I MISS NY
Shown here is a typographic painting created for the Ace Hotel, New York. The lettering was hand-painted with acrylic paints. (Photograph by Davi Russo.)

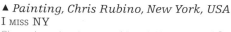

▲ *Merchandise, Marion Deuchars and Angus Hyland of Pentagram, London, UK*
YOUNG BRITISH ARTIST / LET'S FILL THIS BOOK WITH ART / LET'S FILL THIS BOOK WITH DRAWING
The type for this project, used on a variety of materials, was created for London-based art store chain Cass Art Kids.

▶ *Book, Lisa Rienermann, Berlin, Germany*

IF I COULD WISH FOR MYSELF THEN I MIGHT WISH FOR MY, OUR FAVORITE AND MOST FAMILIAR MEAL

Rienermann used a semi-permanent marker to write on to porcelain, which was then photographed and put together in a booklet.

▲ *Poster, Erik Buckham, Los Angeles, USA*

FLIGHT OF THE CONCHORDS: BACK 2 BUSINESS TIME

The lettering featured on this poster was hand-drawn; the poster was art-directed by Jon Manheim.

▲ *Poster, Erik Buckham, Los Angeles, USA*

FLIGHT OF THE CONCHORDS: SEASON 2 DROPPING SOON

The inspiration for this was 1970s TV shows and children's theater. The text was hand-drawn, then scanned ready for layout.

▲ *Poster, Adam Hayes, London, UK*

ALL THE LIVES I COULD LIVE, ALL THE PEOPLE I WILL NEVER KNOW, NEVER WILL BE, THEY ARE EVERYWHERE

The type on this poster was hand-drawn using pencil on paper. The quote is from Aleksander Hemon's *The Lazarus Project* and the typography aims to reflect the nature of the book.

GALLERY

▲ *Greeting card, Jessie Ford
(represented by Central
Illustration Agency), Brighton, UK*
WISHING YOU A JOYOUS NEW YEAR!
This dove card was complied using
a combination of collage and hand-
drawing techniques before being
scanned and finished in Photoshop.

▲ *Illustration, Alice Stevenson,
London, UK*
ALL THINGS ARE QUITE SILENT
This hand-drawn lettering was created
using a fine liner on paper.

▲ *Illustration, Adam Hayes,
London, UK*
LIVE IN THE WOODS
The letters were drawn by hand,
using ink on paper, then scanned and
manipulated in Photoshop to create
the finished piece.

◀ *Illustration, Alina Günter,
Zürich, Switzerland*
WITHOUT CUSTOMERS IF NECESSARY
Created for Erik Spiekermann's column
in the magazine *Form*. It was hand-drawn,
using a fine liner on paper.

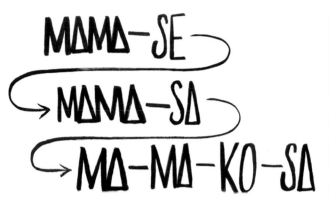

▲ *Illustration, J. Zachary Keenan, Minneapolis, USA*
MAMA-SE, MAMA-SA, MA-MA-KO-SA
Words from the 1970s hit single "Soul Makossa" inspired this piece, which was created using paint on paper.

▲ *Single cover, Dan Abbott, Berlin, Germany*
BABA OTTOKAR
The lettering for this album cover was created in line with the illustration, also featured on the cover. All lettering was hand-drawn before being colored in Photoshop.

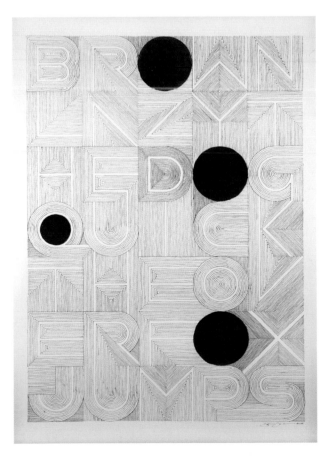

◄ *Poster, Steve Alexander at Rinzen, Australia/ USA/Germany*
THE QUICK BROWN FOX JUMPS OVER THE LAZY DOG
The lettering for this poster was hand-drawn using ink on paper. Alexander purposely took the liberty of undermining the legibility of this common phrase by dissecting the linear construction of each letter, using repeated lines.

▲ *Book cover, Fanny Bostrom, Brooklyn, USA*
JAMES AND THE GIANT PEACH
The lettering for this book cover was made by hand, using gouache on paper.

GALLERY

▲ *Painting, Chris Rubino,
New York, USA*
EITHER
This typographic painting was
created for a room in the Ace
Hotel, New York. The lettering
was hand-painted, using
acrylic pens. (Photograph
by Davi Russo.)

▶ *Poster, Sarah King
of Evening Tweed,
London, UK*
Various phrases
This poster was part of
the *Pick Me Up* exhibition
at Somerset House. King
sketched a rough layout for
the poster by hand, before
drawing in the lettering.

▲ *Illustration, Mia Nolting, Portland, USA*
THINK ABOUT NOTHING
The concept behind this lettering was to create*
letterforms within negative space to show how
"nothing" can create "something."

▲ *Illustration, Alina Günter, Zürich, Switzerland*
DO YOU REMEMBER?
Inspired by old, wooden cottages, this geometric type
was created using pencil on paper.

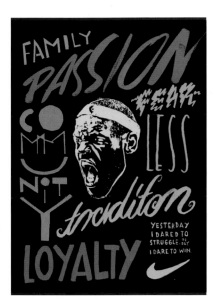

▲ *Poster, Alex Jahn of USE USE,*
Cologne, Germany
BIG LOVE: CLUESO, DENDEMANN,
GYPSIES & CURSE
The lettering for this poster was hand
drawn in black ink, and then scanned and
colored in Photoshop.

▲ *Poster, Stuart Whitton,*
Neath, UK
MY HEART BEATS FOR THIS
Whitton shaped the letters for this
poster using strips of material, before
photographing and printing them. He
then drew the letters by hand, in pencil
on paper, to create the final piece.

▲ *Poster, Sebastian Haslauer,*
Berlin, Germany
FAMILY, PASSION, COMMUNITY, TRADITION,
LOYALTY, FEARLESS. YESTERDAY I DARED
TO STRUGGLE. TODAY I DARE TO WIN
Haslauer hand-drew this type to
illustrate the meaning of the words.
His design was adjusted and finished
in Adobe Photoshop.

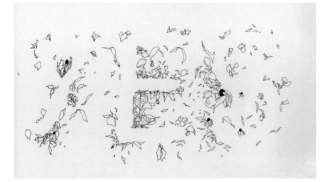

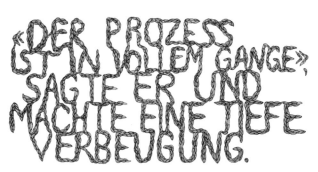

▲ *Illustration, Mia Nolting, Portland, USA*
YES
Hand-drawn shapes are arranged to create the word
"Yes" within the negative space of this piece.

▲ *Illustration, Alina Günter, Zürich, Switzerland*
"THE PROCESS IS IN FULL SWING," HE SAID, AND TOOK A DEEP BOW.
This type, for Birkhäuser Verlag, was created using a fine liner
on paper, then scanned and colored in InDesign.

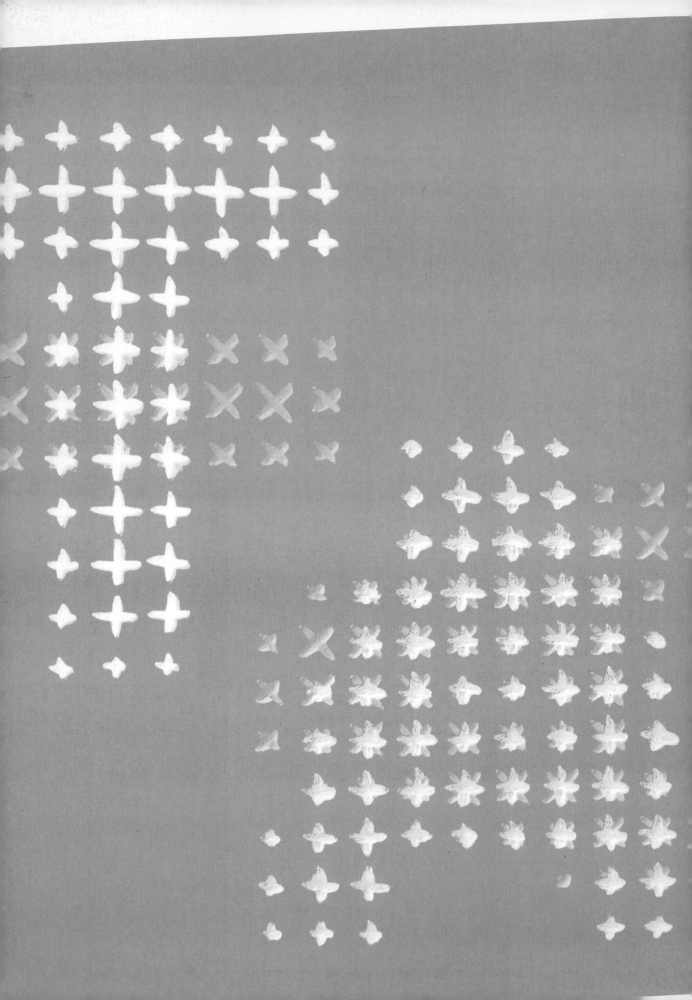

Chapter 2:
Printed, stitched, or cut

Moving away from using a pen or pencil on paper, many designers and creatives enjoy exploring alternative methods and media in which to create type or lettering for a given design project. While not every design brief will allow for such experimentation, if it does then there are many different avenues to explore, from sewn or stitched lettering, to papercut type, to type created using tape. UK designer Smart Emma creates many different works through the stitched medium, often creating words within the negative space created by her stitches (see pages 50–51). The popularity in papercutting sees no sign of abating with the growth in popularity of designers such as MrYen who creates type for his work by cutting the letters in paper using a scalpel (see pages 62–65). Also in this chapter are examples of type created using potato printing (see page 77) and even corrugated cardboard, both of which make for great end results.

PROFILE Smart Emma

Lancashire, UK

Smart Emma is from the northwest of England and works as a graphic designer by day and a crafter by night. The crafting side of her life is encouraged by the fact that she enjoys creating visual, tactile projects that emphasize the craft in the making of them.

Emma works with a number of different materials to create her projects, including embroidery silks, wool, mesh, cardboard, material, and cotton. "When I was at university studying graphic design, I covered a wide range of aspects and experimented with different materials," she explains. "My most memorable was an installation that I created to inspire designers to be more creative, away from their computers. Some of the objects included sketchbook desks, RGB paint dispensers, iMac magna-doodle, and a cardboard parquet floor that you could draw on." This love of materials continued into her professional life. "I like the textures and colors that the wool and embroidery silks create. These effects have to be handcrafted and cannot be created on the computer. I like the way my projects take time to create and how each piece becomes an original in its own right."

▲ *Cushion*
NIGHTY NIGHT
This embroidered type is made using glow-in-the-dark thread to create cushions. When the piece is viewed in the dark, the cushions glow and create words.

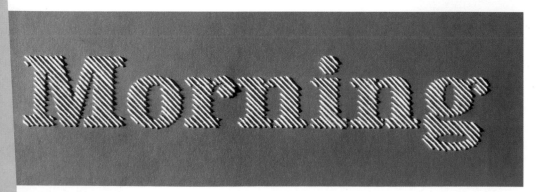

◄ ▲ *Card*
MORNING
This is a personal project to create different greetings, using a range of craft techniques. This one was produced using thread and card.

Inspired by anything and everything, Emma is always on blogs and looking in magazines and books for inspiration. "What I love about being a graphic designer is that it's a job that lets me be so creative every day—fair enough, there are restraints, but that just makes it more challenging," she says. "The type that I design allows me to be quite experimental and different, and that's why I like it."

▲ *Sign detail*
Emma used the mesh squares to create a pattern for the type.

◄ *Sign*
SORRY WE'RE CLOSED
This idea was borne from traditional open and closed signs found in stores. Smart Emma created this version using wool and mesh.

CHARACTER CREATION *Printed, Stitched, or Cut*

TUTORIAL Smart Emma

Lancashire, UK

Emma's Hello type was the first type she created for her portfolio. "I wanted a way to show my craftier side and thought this would be a nice opening to my portfolio when I had a job interview—a bit different and, hopefully, memorable," she explains. The type was created using a Helvetica typeface stencil as a base. Emma then gradually built up the tiny stitched dots around the stencil to reveal the word "Hello." In the finished project, the stitches are more tightly bunched toward the center and more widely spaced farther away from the lettering.

▲ HELLO

INGREDIENTS

· Printout of text/image
· Carbon paper
· Material
· Pen
· Embroidery hoop
· Needle
· Embroidery silk
· Scissors

Step 1
Print out your chosen word, then cut a piece of carbon paper and place this between the material and printout.

Step 2
Carefully trace over the text. If necessary, use a few pins to hold the paper in place so that it doesn't shift while you trace on it.

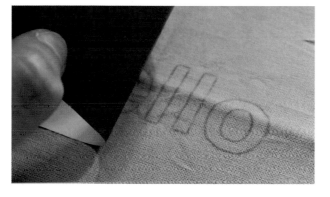

Step 3
Remove the printout and carbon paper and stretch the material into the embroidery hoop.

Step 4
Using the traced outline, start to sew around the text, building up the stitches to make a fairly thick printed outline.

Step 5
Here, small stitches are used to give the effect of tiny grains. You could use longer stitches or knots to create different effects.

Step 6
Try to sew around the basic outline first, making sure you have stitched around the entire pattern, before adding stitches to fill in your design.

PROFILE Evelin Kasikov

Tallinn, Estonia / London, UK

Kasikov specializes in typographic illustration, handmade graphics, and editorial and book design. She is hugely influenced by modernist design principles, geometry, and grid systems. "My work is an intriguing combination of something very precise, technology, and something very accidental, handmade craft," she explains. "My distinctive approach to typography is based on what I would describe as 'analytical craft,' rational and analytical work in combination with handmade techniques. I am interested in the relationship between seeing, reading, and writing, and what kind of new experiences a handmade approach can create on a printed page."

Despite creating much of her work using embroidery, Kasikov does not work freehand. Her embroidered pieces are extremely precise. All elements are carefully measured and calculated. She likes to experiment with the technical side of her work: with grids, order, format, sizes, and spaces. "I do not do many sketches," she explains, "rather, when working on a commissioned piece, I usually write down two or three possible directions and then allow myself time to think about them. It is important for me to give myself this time to think.

◄ *Illustration detail*
Q
The idea was to explore handmade CMYK overprints in the context of type. This was Kasikov's first full hand-stitched alphabet.

▲ *Illustration*
Alphabet
Kasikov's CMYK alphabet was created for *UPPERCASE* magazine. It consists of 26 sans serif, uppercase letterforms on a grid of 5 x 5in (12 x 12cm). Each letter is hand embroidered using a combination of two overlapping CMYK colors.

► *Poster*

YOUR TENTSHIP, YOUR AZURENESS, YOUR CORNFLOWER BLUE
This poster was created for a group exhibition called Sprung held at Fedrigoni, London. Kasikov used cross-stitch to create the words. The work is full of color, leaving the words to show in the negative space on the paper.

"Once I've decided what to do, the process is quick. I create the grids on-screen and then stitch." Kasikov sees her work very much as Estonian. "I think my background is an important part of my work," she adds. "The way that I use handmade techniques reflects our strong craft tradition.

"Being located on the border of Eastern and Western Europe, Estonia has a combination of different cultural influences, from Scandinavian to Russian to ancient Finno-Ugric."

TUTORIAL Evelin Kasikov

Tallinn, Estonia / London, UK

The idea behind this typeface was to create an experimental alphabet that would bring together modular and geometric letterforms and handmade techniques, and to experiment with optical illusions and the handmade form. How do we see letters and how does the tactile technique affect perception? The letters of this type appear three-dimensional not only because of design, but also because of the tactile surface. The creation of this type makes use of both digital and hand-crafted media, beginning life in InDesign and being finished by hand using a needle and thread.

INGREDIENTS

- Paper of your choice
- Awl
- Cotton thread
- Embroidery needles
- Scissors

▲ Alphabet

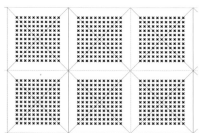

Step 1

First, create a cross of size ⅛ x ⅛in (3 x 3mm), then prepare a matrix of 11 x 11 crosses. The grid can consist of any number of square modules but smaller grids are harder to work with because you have more limited options.

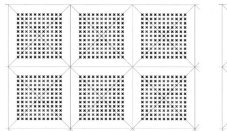

Step 2

Create modular letterforms on the grid with equal widths (two lines) and proportions.

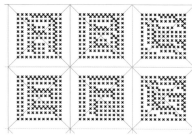

Step 3

Once all the letterforms are complete, move them slightly so as to create a 3D effect.

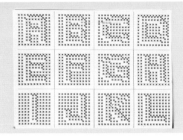

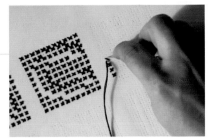

Step 4
Print off the prepared artwork, which is now ready to be stitched.

Step 5
Place your design as a worksheet on paper and then mark out the letterforms using an awl ready for stitching.

Step 6
Split the thread, so you are using three threads. Begin to stitch the letters following the letterforms that you marked out with the awl.

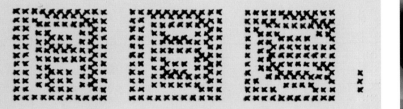

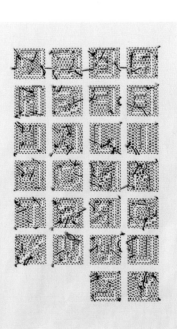

Step 7
You could work with single crosses, creating one full cross at a time, or you could make a row of half-crosses in one direction and then another row back to complete the crosses

Step 8
To finish, run the thread under several stitches, so that it is safely secured and will not come undone.

Step 9
The finished letterforms clearly show the desired double-3D effect.

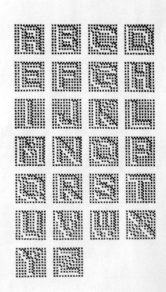

PROFILE James Hancock

Sydney, Australia / New York, USA

Hancock describes himself as a visual artist, illustrator, and animator. His work has appeared in major print, TV, and music publishing releases around the world, and has been exhibited internationally. He has traveled widely and participated in projects in Indonesia, Austria, Germany, France, the USA, UK, and Australia. Currently based in Brooklyn, he is aiming to draw every building in New York. "I'm inspired by psychology, science, and philosophy… I've been designing and creating typefaces since I was very young. I remember as a kid I used to trace fonts from books when I was in primary school. It has always been a passion," he says.

Hancock specializes in creating whimsical hand-drawn imagery and typography. He works mainly by hand, using different materials and media, including pencil and pen on paper, and sometimes collage.

▶ *Illustration*
JAMES GULLIVER HANCOCK
This piece was created as a self-promotional card for Hancock and is inspired by the psychology and physics of how we see. It was hand-drawn before being scanned and finished in Photoshop.

▶ *Print*
BLUE MURDER MONGRELS
This limited-edition print was created by Hancock for an exhibition about the history of "the neighborhood" that was held in Sydney, Australia. He chose 1970s Chippendale, an inner-city suburb that was crime-ridden at that time. All the lettering was hand-drawn by Hancock.

◀ *CD Poster*
Snippets of lyrics
Hancock created this pullout CD poster for musician Lenka. "The idea with this was to create a colorful exploration of Lenka's lyrics, creating a sense of it taking place in a world of its own," explains Hancock, "where animals, words, and colors mix."

▲ Posters
Snippets of lyrics
This series of limited-edition posters was created for musician, Lenka. Hancock wanted to create posters that guided the viewer through Lenka's lyrics.

His work is then often scanned into Photoshop, in which he manipulates the levels, adds color, and arranges the different elements to create a final piece.

His clients include magazine publishers, book publishers, music industry clients, and advertising agencies. "I really love seeing the characters that I have created appear on some form of communication, it is what I always wanted to do and I enjoy it very much," he says. "I particularly enjoy creating type by hand, as it is like an extension of your handwriting but in lots of different forms. It is really satisfying to personalize language like this and evolve it into something new." As well as hand-drawing type and letters, Hancock likes to print and stencil (see tutorial overleaf), which, he finds, adds another level to creating handmade type. "With spraying and other printing like etching and silkscreen you often get little marks and ink spots that, although unexpected, can be really great," he explains. "It's like a controlled chaos, which really makes sense to me."

▶ Illustrations
Prize, 1st, win, totally delicious, gold, silver, tasty, top 10, nice, winner, first / Fantasy, wink wink!, secret, confession
These two editorial illustrations were hand-drawn and finished in Photoshop.

TUTORIAL James Hancock

Sydney, Australia / New York, USA

This poster, created by Hancock in his studio in The Pencil Factory, Greenpoint, Brooklyn, very much involves getting your hands dirty. As Hancock says: "I love having dirty hands… Spray-paint stencils and printing in general are really fun because of all the little mistakes you get. You get a whole lot of character from those mistakes." Old-style circus posters inspired the design of this poster. However, you could use the same principles to create variations on this. You will need either a large indoor space or a dry outdoor space for this project.

INGREDIENTS

- Three sheets of paper
- Pencil
- Craft knife
- Cutting mat
- Two colors of spray paint

► COMING SOON

Step 1
Draw out the words you want to print in a thick, hand-drawn font—don't worry if it's messy.

Step 2
Cut out the letters you have drawn with the craft knife. Don't worry about cutting the holes in the centers of letters.

Step 3
Place this stencil on one of the other sheets of paper that you have and then use one of the colors of spray paint to spray the stenciled letters.

Step 4
Using the guide print you've just made, draw in all the details for the letters—the underlines, dots, stars, and so on.

Step 5
Cut out the details that you have just drawn on the sheet.

Step 6
Take the last sheet of fresh paper that you have and put the first cut-out stencil on it, then spray it with your first color.

Step 7
Remove the first stencil and replace it with the second cut-out stencil you made featuring all the details.

Step 8
Spray the second chosen color on top of the first. Remove the last stencil and you're done. Now you can make as many posters as you need!

TUTORIAL Tyrone Ohia

Wellington, New Zealand

◀ SCARED OF THE
DARK; AMUSING
WORD MESSAGE
BY NIGHT

AMUSING WORD
MESSAGE BY NIGHT

INGREDIENTS

- Paper
- Light box

"The creation of this type is an exercise in chance and serendipity," explains designer Tyrone Ohia. "I was trying to make textile patterns by dragging random objects along the photocopier and then I started making overlay patterns on the light box. Through some twist of fate, I arranged the overlapping objects into the shape of an 'H' and the rest is history." Once the H was created, Ohia went on to fold paper in order to make all the letters of the alphabet. Ohia also created different variations on this theme, including Normal Norman, Wide Load, Sky Scraper, and Hit the Slopes. "Every time I make a letter I just plunge straight in and fold and tear where I want," he says. "The result is a sort of snowflake typeface, every letter is different every time."

Step 1
To create the letter A, first fold the paper in half.

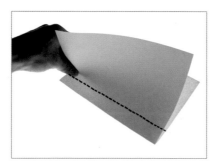

Step 2
Refold the paper over the first fold, so that you overlay the paper.

Step 3
Now you have the crossbar of the letter A.

Step 4

To create the stems, fold in one side of the paper to create another overlay.

Step 5

Now fold the opposite side to create the second stem— this creates the letter H.

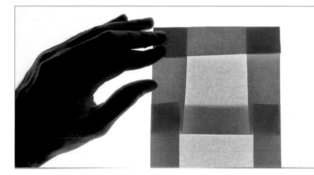

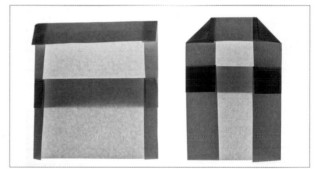

Step 6

Simply fold over the top edge of the paper to complete the letter A.

Step 7

Now you know the technique, you can experiment with the widths, heights, and type of corners of your letter A.

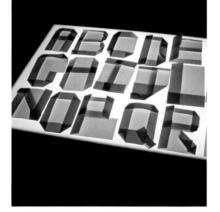

Step 8

You can now go on to create all the letters of the alphabet using your light box. (This is where a larger light box comes in handy.)

Step 9

Different letters throw up different challenges. For instance, an L is fairly straightforward but J and Q require more thought. In this instance the tail of the Q has been created by ripping a small piece of paper and overlaying it on the folded sheet of paper. The V has been created with multiple folds.

PROFILE MrYen

Leeds, UK

MrYen, otherwise known as Jonathan Chapman, specializes in hand-cut paper artwork and stationery. Since his graduation he has built up his freelance career, taking on specially commissioned work and selling his custom line, both direct to customers as well as in art galleries and craft stores. "I started to create papercut artwork as I wanted an alternative method of illustrating and I have always loved paper, so this seemed the obvious next step," he explains. "The need to explore paper to its full potential keeps me experimenting, as there are so many things you can do with paper."

▲ *Papercut display*
HAPPY FRIDAY!
This papercut is part of a series experimenting with typography and imagery. A new design was made every Friday for several months by Chapman.

◄ *Postcard*
HANSEL & GRETEL
These postcards are part of a series of hand-cut paper postcards, taking inspiration from fairytales.

► *Papercut display*
READ THE DIRECTIONS AND DIRECTLY YOU WILL BE DIRECTED IN THE RIGHT DIRECTION
This papercut sees design mixing natural forms with typography. The quote used is from *Alice's Adventures In Wonderland*.

◄▲ *Papercut display*
A MISTAKE IS SIMPLY
ANOTHER WAY OF
DOING THINGS
This is an experimental
hand-cut paper design
that keeps the counters
in the typography, while
cutting away the rest
of the character.

Inspired by repetitive patterns in nature, manmade patterns, travel, typography, vintage food labels, postal ephemera, and traditional typefaces, Chapman works on his Mac creating designs, which he then prints off and cuts by hand using a blade. "I enjoy working freelance as I have the freedom to choose the projects I work on and how I go about completing them… I love working with typography and image together, but I have a real love for the simple shapes and the ways that letterforms can be used," he explains. "I find it interesting to view letters and characters as shapes and objects, rather than purely tools for communication. I find this greatly helps with my creativity and it definitely affects how I create a typographic papercut."

► *Papercut quote*
SCIENCE HAS MADE
US GODS EVEN BEFORE
WE ARE WORTHY OF
BEING MEN.
This is a hand-cut
design, with science
being the topic of
focus. The quote is
by Jean Rostand.

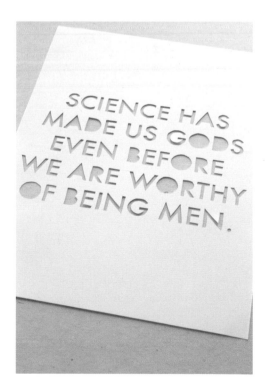

TUTORIAL MrYen

Leeds, UK

Chapman began by selecting a quote to use. This one comes from Ralph Waldo Emerson: "Adopt the pace of nature: her secret is patience." He then created a layout template, using the quote in Illustrator, before printing out the file ready to create the papercut. The idea was to create a piece that featured simple, bold typography, with a floral flourish. The typography has been adapted in specific places where certain letterforms are too close to each other to cut individually. In addition, the counters of the font have all been removed to make the papercut easier to work with.

▶ ADOPT THE PACE OF NATURE: HER SECRET IS PATIENCE.

INGREDIENTS

· Illustrator
· Template
· Lightweight paper
· Scalpel
· Craft mat

Step 1
Using reference material on which you want to base your papercut, create a design in Illustrator that you feel works with your chosen theme and manipulate the typography and imagery to reflect this.

Step 2
Turn your typography to outlines and remove the counters from each character (this makes it easier to know what to cut later).

Step 3

Secure the template to your chosen paper with paper clips.

Step 4

Cut the detailed, delicate bits of the design first, as you could accidentally cut something off. This avoids ruining all your hard work.

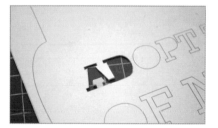

Step 5

Next, cut the smallest and most detailed sections of the typography. Where certain characters are quite close, they could be cut together as one shape, giving them a quirky-looking finish.

Step 6

Cut the curved characters first, as these will be difficult to cut once more of the paper has been removed. Move the paper around, not your hand, as this gives greater control over the scalpel.

Step 7

Always use the tip of the blade to enter an angular area that is next to a delicate part of the design and cut away from, instead of toward, the delicate area.

Step 8

Check for any areas of paper that have not been cut through properly; they can look unsightly. Take your scalpel and use short, stabbing motions to remove the problem area swiftly and neatly.

Step 9

Mount the final papercut. A quick and easy method is to use a spray adhesive. Your papercut is now ready to frame.

PROFILE Mathilde Nivet

Paris, France

Nivet began to work with paper when she was studying at the Duperré public art school in Paris. She has since become one of the most prolific designers working in the increasingly popular area of papercraft today, with clients such as Timberland, Petit Bateau, Citroën, *Le Monde*, and Hazan Editions.

She is largely inspired by Japanese art but, as she explains, many other things give her ideas and inspiration. "I observe children and the way they naturally and constantly create virtual or real spaces, images, and things," she says. "Living in a big city like Paris is also a massive inspiration. The way people look, shops, galleries, and so on … whenever I go for a walk, I come back with new ideas."

◄ *Window display*
EARTHKEEPER
Cardboard letters created by Nivet for Timberland's Paris store. The inspiration behind the piece was discovery.

▲ *Letter display*
N
This N was created for an exhibition. The N sits inside floral elements, which have been hand-cut using a scalpel and paper that has a white side and an orange side.

◄ *Window display*
ORIGAMI JEWELLERY
These 3D card letters
were created for
a window display
for Rainbow Origami
Jewellery. The type
used was originally
created for the brand
by the typographer
Patrick Paleta.

▼ *Papercut quote*
HE WHO THINKS VERY
LITTLE MAKES LOTS
OF MISTAKES
This is one of Nivet's
trademark typographic
papercuts, this time
featuring a quote from
Leonardo da Vinci.

Working with paper, using scissors and
a craft knife, Nivet has worked on many and
varied projects, from invitations to window
installations. "I love to work on many different
projects and often do, so one day is never
the same," she explains. "I love that I am
asked to be creative, it's a great opportunity,
you get to do something useful and at the
same make the reader think or laugh, just
looking at the letters."

TUTORIAL Mathilde Nivet

Paris, France

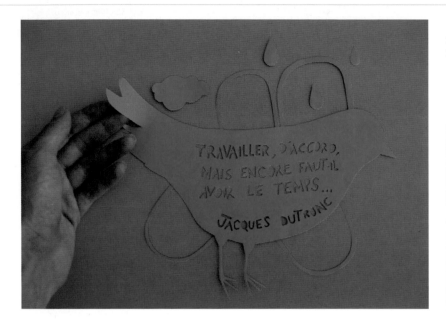

INGREDIENTS

- Pencil
- Letter paper in one color
- Scissors
- Craft knife
- Craft mat
- Eraser
- Blu-Tack
- Ledger paper in another color
- Camera

Shown here is a papercut that was created for publishers Hazan Editions. The brief was to create a fun, decorative papercut with text that was easily read from a long distance. The quotation is from Jacques Dutronc, the famous 1960s French singer. "The idea with this piece was to create something simple and elegant, which is why I choose to use only two colors within the design," explains Nivet. "I decided to feature a bird as the main element within which I would cut out the required letters. I started by drawing a few sketches of birds and experimenting with different nature-inspired elements around it before deciding on the final design. From here I began to cut and assemble the design, trying different combinations as I went." The final piece features clouds and rain in reference to the sky, and the curves aim to interpret the waves of music.

Step 1

Begin by sketching out your bird shape on the blue sheet. Then draw the different decorative elements around the bird, making sure to leave space between them. Always draw more elements than you need so you have choice when you get to the composing stage.

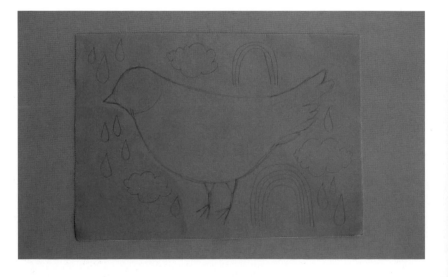

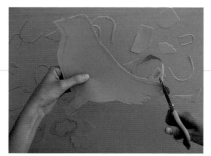

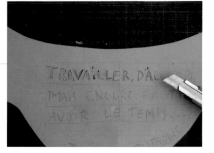

Step 2

Using the scissors, cut out all the elements. Start by roughly cutting the outline of all the different elements, then cut them to shape more precisely. Be sure to concentrate, as this is the real drawing stage—you are using the scissors to draw by making sharp, precise graphic forms appear.

Step 3

When the shape is complete, turn the bird over and, taking your pencil, lightly draw out the letters that you are going to cut.

Step 4

Using your craft knife, carefully cut out the letters. Always start with the most fragile part and the shortest parts, taking your time. Make sure you keep your craft knife sharp at all times, replacing the blade when necessary.

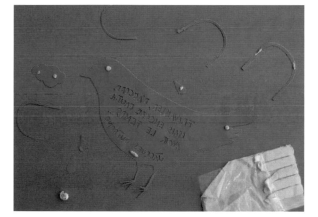

Step 5

When you have cut out all your letters, take your eraser and gently remove any remaining trace of pencil. Make sure you keep the paper flat with your free hand to prevent it crumpling or ripping.

Step 6

Once complete, turn every element over and fix a little Blu-Tack to each. This helps secure the paper and also raises the papercuts, creating a slight shadow that gives your final image some depth.

Step 7

Position the different elements, as required, on the background paper. Once you are happy with your arrangement, push gently on the paper to make the Blu-Tack stick and then raise some of the corners to create more shadow. You are now ready to photograph your work. Use Adobe Photoshop to change the colors, framing, or light, if required.

✱ TIPS

When photographing your work be sure to position yourself directly above the papercut. Natural daylight is the best light in which to photograph paper, so try to shoot on a bright, sunny day (if possible).

PROFILE Amy Borrell
Melbourne, Australia

We Make Words is a blog about all things lettering and type run by illustrator and designer Amy Borrell and illustrator Luci Everett. The idea is that they take it in turns to photograph a word made of anything from paper to ribbon to wood to straws. Each new word somehow relates to the last and is posted as an image on the blog. "I love creating lettering or type outside of the computer; constructing something physical and spontaneous is great fun," she explains.

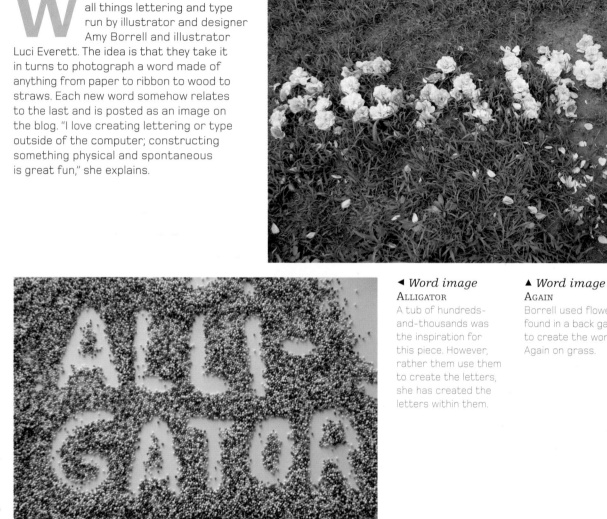

◄ *Word image*
ALLIGATOR
A tub of hundreds-and-thousands was the inspiration for this piece. However, rather them use them to create the letters, she has created the letters within them.

▲ *Word image*
AGAIN
Borrell used flowers found in a back garden to create the word Again on grass.

◄ *Word image*
CHOCOLATE
Using a selection of pastel-colored paper tape, Borrell has ripped pieces off to create the word Chocolate.

► *Word image*
CHUCKLES
Borrell used the mini
wooden clothespins
that she had at home
to create the word
Chuckles.

As well as running the We Make Words project, Borrell also as works as a freelance designer and illustrator under the name of Cake With Giants on a variety of design projects, including book, exhibition, and product design. "I love to create projects that have some sort of silly, whimsical element," she explains. "I create all sorts of different things for clients in fashion, publishing, music, and retail, as well as illustrating patterns for fabric, clothing prints, and also for magazines." Inspired by childhood, storytellers, and possibility, Borrell will work in whatever medium she thinks suits the project she is working on, as long as the approach is "playful and filled with its own narrative." She tends to create her illustrations using watercolors and gray, lead pencil but, as can be seen with her We Make Words project, she will work with almost anything.

▲ *Word image*
EAT
Carefully arranged
fairy lights taped
to a wall, then
photographed
with the lights out
create the word Eat.

► *Word image*
SWEET
Colored sewing pins
were used to form
a frame around which
to wrap a thin length
of wool to create the
word Sweet.

TUTORIAL Amy Borrell

Melbourne, Australia

◄ Alphabet

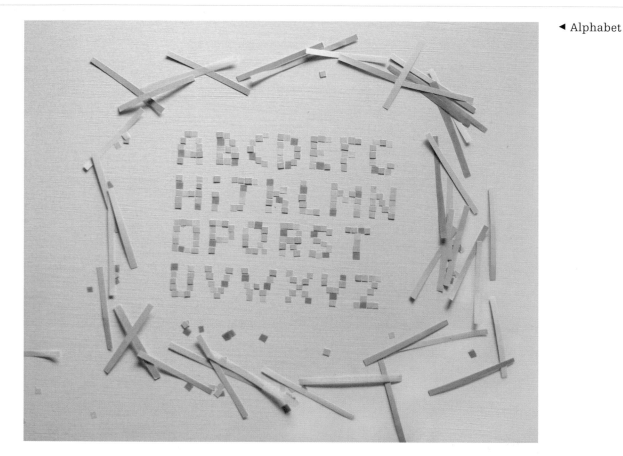

We Make Words began as a project to allow Borrell and Everett to break away from their desks and computers, and experiment with different materials. Objects are arranged to create each word and then photographed and posted on the We Make Words blog. "We usually make our words with whatever is at hand at the time," explains Borrell, "and they usually take no more than half an hour to complete. The idea is that the words and how we make them are quick and spontaneous."

INGREDIENTS

· Paper scraps in various colors
· Scissors
· Camera
· Adobe Photoshop

Step 1

Cut your paper into even strips that are around ¼in (5mm) wide. To create larger letters, simply cut larger strips.

Step 2
Next, cut the strips into little squares. These can be rough as the idea is that this is handmade, and so doesn't need to be perfect. Aim for an equal amount of squares in the various different colors.

Step 3
Working on a clean, flat surface, arrange the squares into letterforms. These letters are approximately 5in (12cm) high by 3–4in (7–10cm) wide.

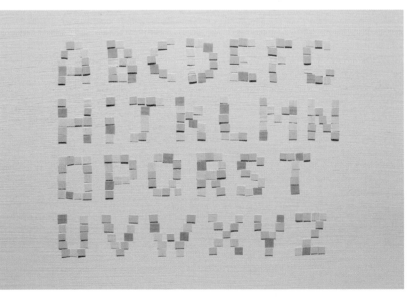

Step 5
When finished, decorate your alphabet with any leftover strips. Photograph, import into Adobe Photoshop, and use your letters however you like.

Step 4
Continue arranging the squares to create letters until you have laid out the entire alphabet. The distribution of squares doesn't need to be exact, but try to keep a balance throughout.

GALLERY

▲ *Logo, Airside, London, UK*
GREENPEACE PRESENTS AIRPLOT! STOP HEATHROW EXPANSION
The type for this logo was developed using the old-school technique of printing using paint and letters cut out of cardboard.

▲ *Illustration, Alex Robbins, London, UK*
BRANDS
This involved creating a set of small, stenciled people by cutting the shapes out of card. Three different colors were then applied to the shapes using ink pads. The shapes were then carefully placed and pressed on to paper. They were arranged with the people surrounding the negative space.

▲ *Book cover, Working Format, Vancouver, Canada*
DRIFTER
Instead of printing or stamping the letters onto these book covers, the designers opted for stitching the letters on by hand.

▲ *Album cover, Handverk, Oslo, Norway*
PETTER CARLSEN
This album cover was created for artist Petter Carlsen, who is signed to EMI Music. The idea was to create something different and so the type was created using cross-stitch.

▲ *Leafcut, Charlotte Lord, London, UK*
INSTRUCTION BOOK
Lord cut letters into a leaf using a scalpel.

▶ *Papercut, Alex Robbins, London, UK*
FRAGILE
A self-initiated project created using white paper and a hole punch. "Often ideas come from old work, which I keep in a folder and use when the time is right," Robbins explains.

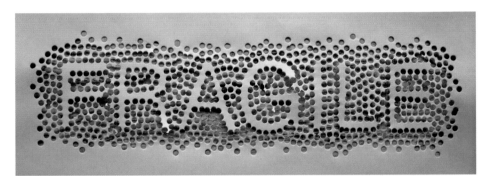

▶ *Illustration, Yulia Brodskaya, St Albans, UK*
INSTANT
Brodskaya's brief from coffee chain Starbucks was to create an exuberant paper lettering piece to promote the store's instant coffee.

◀ *Display, Martin Pyper of Me Studio, Amsterdam, the Netherlands*
Alphabet
Pyper created Pokerface using a pack of cards and a pair of scissors. He began by cutting out the letters E and M to set the necessary dimensions before continuing with the rest of the alphabet. He also created a selection of glyphs and numbers.

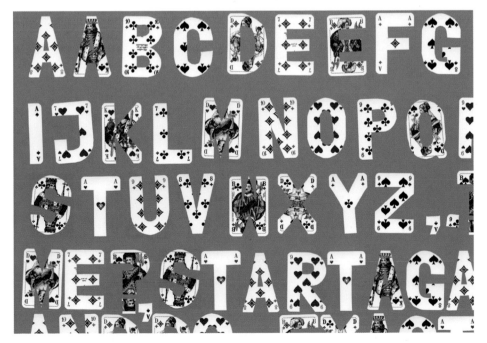

GALLERY

◄ *Mural, Rob and Barry van Dijck at Stay Nice, Breda, the Netherlands*
YOU RECOGNIZE THE SMELL, A HOUSE BECOMES HOTEL
This lettering was created from paper, which was cut out and glued onto the wall of an abandoned house.

▲ *Poster, Milkxhake, Hong Kong, China*
PRAY & PAY
In keeping with Chinese tradition, the letters for this poster were created by folding Chinese paper.

▲ *Illustration, Vladimir and Maksim Loginov at Hand Made Font, Tallinn, Estonia*
YOU ARE FAT
This lettering was created using folded paper.

▲ *Illustration, Yulia Brodskaya, St Albans, UK*
WHO'S WHO
Designed for *The Knitter* magazine, the idea was to create a paper illustration and lettering in the form of a ball of knitting yarn.

▲ *Poster, Andrea Zeman, Zagreb, Croatia*
ORIGAMI: THE ART OF PAPER FOLDING
Memories from a childhood making origami characters inspired the creation of this alphabet. Zeman began with sketches, working with paper to create the lettering, which was then digitized.

▶ *Illustration, Yulia Brodskaya, St Albans, UK*
LOOK GOOD
This piece uses Brodskya's trademark cut-and-rolled papercraft technique.

▶ *Poster, Juan Ramon Pastor, Alba Durana, and Alba Jordana, Barcelona, Spain*
CREATIVE MOMENTS: WE ALL HAVE ONE
This poster was designed for an event encouraging people to use handmade techniques. The type was created using the potato printing method.

◀ *Album cover, Inventory, London, UK*
WAKE UP
This lettering was created using folded, white paper, then photographed and imported into Photoshop, ready for use on the album cover.

GALLERY

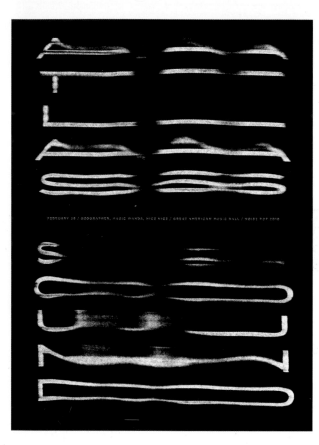

▲► *Greeting cards,*
Christine Föllmer,
Hamburg, Germany
THANK YOU / HAPPY BIRTHDAY
These two sewn greeting
cards are part of a series,
which featured type with
a more personal feel.

▲ *Poster, Jason Munn*
at The Small Stakes,
Oakland, CA, USA
ATLAS SOUND
This poster for Noise Pop
and Atlas Sound reflects
the sometimes eerie and
ghostly nature of the band's
music. Munn started with
Gotham Bold typeface and
then manipulated it on
a photocopier to create
the ghostly effect, before
scanning it back into his
Mac to lay out.

► *Poster, Unfolded,*
Zurich, Switzerland
WHITE TRASH: WE WERE
ALREADY SHIT AS CHILDREN
Fluorescent tape was used
for the main heading on this
poster. Subsequent lettering
was created using Letraset.

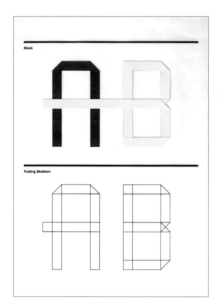

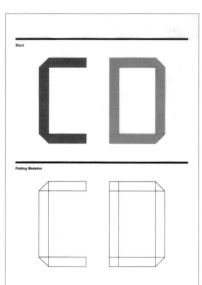

◄ *Poster, Benjamin Koh at Pepper & Cinnamon, Singapore*
A B C D
The folded handles of paper bags inspired this typeface. It began as folded strips of paper and was then digitized to create a complete font.

▲ *Illustration, Jessie Ford, Brighton, UK (represented by Central Illustration Agency)*
Alphabet
This self-promotional piece was created using a mixture of hand-drawn letters and found, cut, and scanned ephemera.

◄ *Illustration, Troy Hyde, London, UK*
D E F J K L
Each letterform for this type was shaped by hand, using corrugated cardboard, and then scanned to create a digital version of the letters.

Chapter 3:

Digitally drawn

Even though the title of this book suggests that the use of digitally drawn type may not be included, some examples of such type demonstrate how the digital can have a handmade aesthetic. Drawing type digitally is a great way for a designer to create lettering and type that is digital yet completely unique. For instance, digitally drawn type can be created by drawing freehand using a mouse, or by drawing on a digital tablet, or, as one example in this chapter shows, by drawing freehand on to the touch screen of an iPad. Some examples in this chapter also show how to take an existing font and modify it digitally by hand. Such options give the designer the opportunity to create a completely new and original type that can easily be made into a complete working font.

PROFILE Natasha Mileshina

Moscow, Russia / New York, USA

Natasha Mileshina established her career as designer and art director in Russia before moving to the USA. She now works for the Metropolitan Museum of Art, and freelances for a number of clients, including *ELLE*, *Afisha*, and *Taste* magazines.

Although she works in all areas of graphic design, Mileshina favors typography and calligraphy. "I love creating type and typography," she explains. "I am free to do whatever I want, literally whatever, which is an amazing feeling." For most of her projects Mileshina combines working on her Mac, using Creative Suite, with working by hand, drawing and sketching. This is evident throughout her work, in which she uses both on- and off-screen techniques. "As well as design, I also work in illustration and photography, which started off as something to complement my design work but now exists as something quite separate, which is good," she explains. "I also run an Etsy shop for which I create posters and prints that feature my hand- or digitally drawn type designs."

▲ *Poster*

I AM SOPHISTICATED
Mileshina's Geometry type was created using modular shapes. "I created five basic shapes and then used them as modules to create different letters," she explains.

▶ *Poster*
LOVE YOU
This lettering was first hand-drawn as a stand-alone piece in Illustrator before being produced as a negative inside a heart shape.

◀ *Poster*
WE MAKE SENSE
This type was created digitally. Mileshina created a cross-stitch module and worked within that to create the letters that she used on this poster for her Etsy shop.

It is clear from much of Mileshina's work that constructivism is a major influence, not least in her Geometry type. "The creation of that type was inspired by El Lissitzky and constructivism as a whole," she says. "It was designed specifically for the phrase 'I Am So Phisticated,' which was then used to create a hip, abstract print for my Etsy shop. I actually came up with the phrase a few years ago while learning English and it took me some time to understand the meaning of the word 'sophisticated'… It was a great word: long, thrilling, and with interesting letters in it, and I played and doodled around with it a lot."

CHARACTER CREATION *Digitally Drawn*

TUTORIAL Natasha Mileshina

Moscow, Russia / New York, USA

Triangle type was created for the Free Encouragement Project, a project aimed at encouraging positivity created by Jeff Hamada of Booooooom and Erin Loechner of Design for Mankind. Mileshina used a sheet of paper with an isometric grid to first sketch and shade in sections to create letterforms, before deciding which ones worked best. She then recreated the letterforms in Adobe Illustrator.

▶ WE MAKE SENSE

INGREDIENTS

- Pencil
- Eraser
- Isometric grid paper
- Adobe Illustrator

Step 1

Start with some sketches on the isometric grid, using pencil and eraser. Try creating different variations of the same letter and then pick the best one.

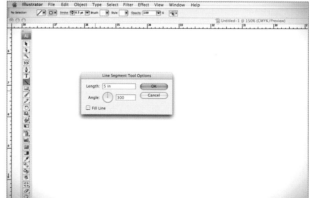

Step 2

Next, recreate the letters on the computer. At first, mimic the isometric grid used as a base. Using the Line Tool in Adobe Illustrator create a few parallel lines with 300° angle.

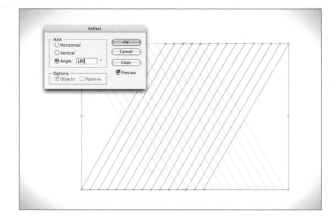

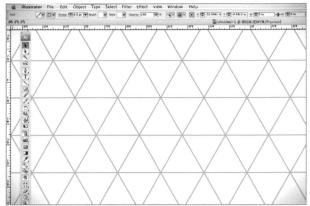

Step 3
Once this is complete, copy and paste these lines and rotate by 180º.

Step 4
Now draw horizontal lines, which can be placed across the angled lines, finalizing your isometric grid. Lock the grid you have made by selecting it and going to Object > Lock > Selection in the upper menu.

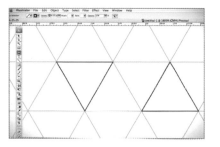

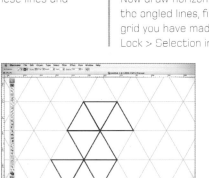

Step 5
Next, create triangles with the Pen Tool to use as modules for building the typeface.

Step 6
Now recreate the letters you sketched before by copying and pasting the triangles. After making all the letters that you need, delete the grid by unlocking it first (Object > Unlock All) and then hitting the "Delete" button.

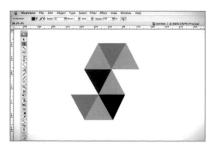

Step 7
After cleaning the Artboard and creating the type composition, color the letters. You can balance the colors better if you start coloring after you have completed your type composition.

Step 8
The complete alphabet. Each letter has a different balance of color, but together they form a unified whole.

CHARACTER CREATION *Digitally Drawn*

PROFILE Honey Design

Sleepy Hollow, USA

Honey Design was set up, and is run, by Rina Miele. The studio specializes in typography, web, logo, and identity design, and clients include Atlantic Records, Umbro, Waterpik, Comcast, and Rubbermaid.

Miele is creating an increasing number of typefaces and wants to continue to do so. "My interest in typography is really growing," she explains. "Amazing typographers like Jessica Hische, Alejandro Paul, or Friends of Type really inspire me. I love creating type and I love that typefaces don't have to be

perfect. They don't have to be expensive. They can just be fun and express what the design is saying to its audience."

In addition to typography Miele has created many interfaces for the web. "For my web work I mostly use Adobe Photoshop from start to finish," she explains. "Logos, typography, or heavy illustration and line work I do in Adobe Illustrator, although of course there are times when a pen, markers, and paper are needed." Miele also runs online font shop I'm a Design Whore.

◄ *Illustration*
Alphabet
Pug was digitally drawn using a Wacom Intuos 4 Stylus. The aim was to achieve an organic, imperfect feel.

▼ ► Sketch
Alphabet
Honey Hand was
hand-drawn using
a trusty Sharpie and
Moleskine. Once Miele
had drawn out the
entire alphabet, she
scanned it and used
Fontographer to
create and export
a font file.

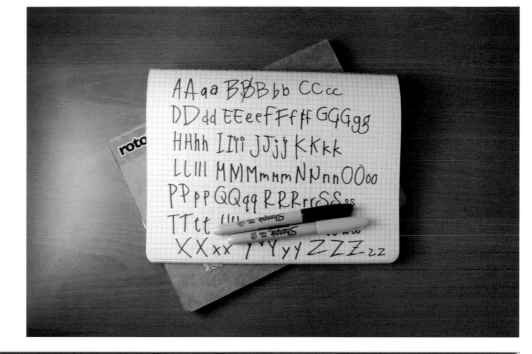

TUTORIAL Honey Design

Sleepy Hollow, USA

Miele describes the creation of this font, using her iPad, as digital finger painting. Using an application called iFontmaker, Miele was able to create and export an entire font in what she describes as a few easy steps. Once you draw the glyphs, you can export a TTF, (fully editable) PDF, or PNG (of composed type) in a matter of minutes. "Using the iPad to create a font is certainly a different way of working, but even though it is digital, you still feel connected to the tangible side of the creation," she explains. "Because it allows you to draw directly onto the screen, you very much feel you have created the font by hand and a few clicks later, it is exported as a font. It is that easy."

INGREDIENTS

- iPad
- iFontmaker app

▲ CLOUD DOODLE

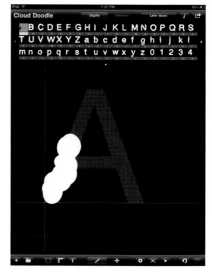

Step 1

When you start up the iFontmaker application you are given a grid view of 62 alphanumeric glyphs. There are multiple grid options and template overlays to get you aligned and even. Click on the top-right button and a drop-down menu will appear. Give your font a name, an author, and edit other kinds of information about the font.

Step 2

The drawing function is smooth and responsive. There aren't too many precise options, such as Bézier curves. Once you make a stroke, there is no real editing and you feel like you really are drawing freehand.

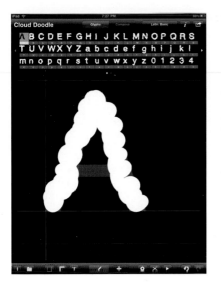 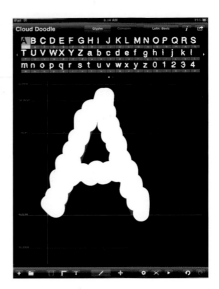

Step 3
Continue drawing out the letter, following the guide letter underneath.

Step 4
This font uses fat strokes to create circular effects. You can adjust the weight of the stroke in the Brush Settings window.

Step 5
Once you have finished the first letter you can now click through to the other glyphs and keep drawing in a circular motion, following the templates. As you work you can see a live preview of your progress at the top of the screen.

Step 6
Once you have finished drawing all the glyphs you can export your font using top-right export icon, ready for use.

PROFILE James Lunn

Southend, UK

James Lunn studied graphic design at the University of Brighton and, whilst there, founded his studio, Memorandom, together with fellow student Michelle Philips. They have since established themselves in the design world working with many clients, including NBC Universal, the Hallmark Channel, Movies 24, and Universal Networks, for whom Lunn installed large-scale typography at a Cannes apartment during the film festival. His design ethos is to explore and experiment. "I tend to work in and out of the computer, I don't rely on one tool, as things can start to look the same. I use scanners, inks, pens, paints, cameras, and broken and unpredictable printers. I like to experiment with processes and enjoy making my own, especially ones that involve the concept of the idea itself, so you can get a really full package as a result. The medium should inform the message." Lunn designs many of his own typefaces when working on projects, and enjoys the process, finding it cathartic and "like solving a code." "When designing a typeface I am usually inspired by an insignificant item in the real world, like a cable clip," he explains. "I'll study it, pull it apart, and rework it into a letterform. I try to approach projects without an expected outcome; I try not to add my ideas to other people's briefs. I like to watch them evolve, informed through good solid research."

ABCDEF
GHIJKLM
NOPQRS
TUVWXYZ

◄ *Illustration*
Alphabet
The idea with this type
was to create a font
inspired by a pencil
and a compass.
It was digitally drawn
in Adobe Illustrator.

► ▼ *Illustration*
MADE / Alphabet
This typeface was
inspired by arcade
games. Lunn created
the type using a grid in
Adobe Illustrator, filling
the squares with three
shades of three colors.

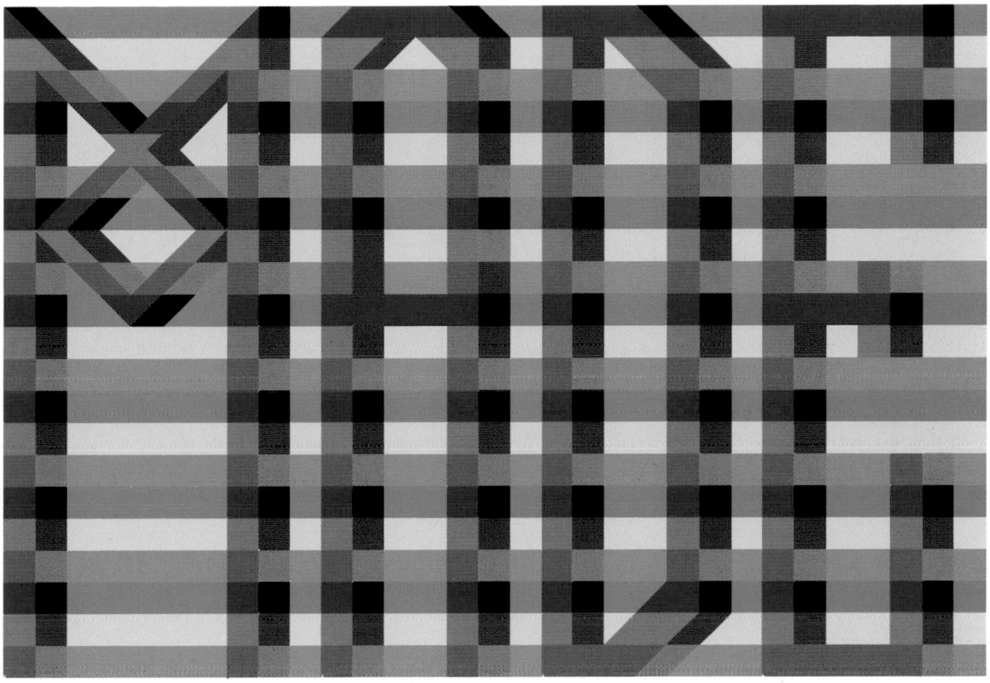

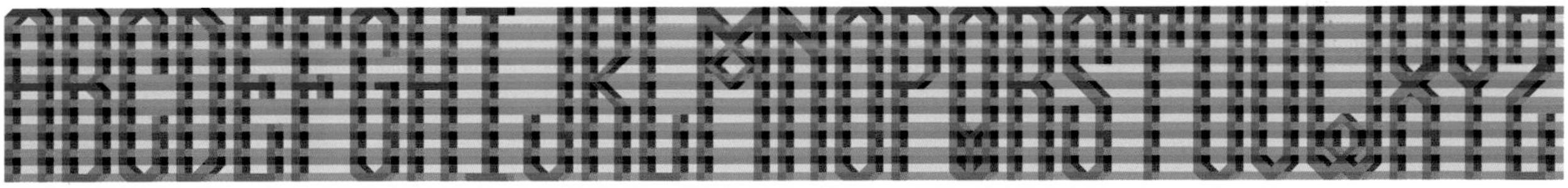

TUTORIAL James Lunn

Southend, UK

Leigh Lights was a "switching on" ceremony for the Christmas lights of Leigh-on-Sea. The type in this promotional poster was inspired by the filaments and shapes in the street lights being used at the event. "This particular year they used new lights, so I wanted to reflect the change in the town's usual Christmas appearance," explains Lunn. "The letterforms reflect the lights used at the event and the colors reflect the atmosphere at that time of year." Lunn created this font in Adobe Illustrator and named it Helena after a friend of his who lived in Leigh at the time.

INGREDIENTS

· Illustrator

▶ NIGHT OF THE LIGHTS: LEIGH LIGHT'S SWITCH-ON, 27 NOVEMBER

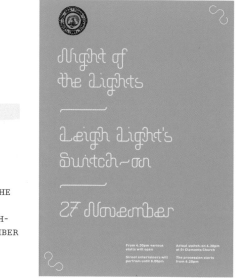

Step 1
Create a new document in Adobe Illustrator (File > New > Document). Using the Pen Tool from the tool bar on the left-hand side, draw a line around 1in (20mm) in length; click where you want the line to start, move the cursor to where you want it to stop, and click again. (Hold Shift when you do this to make the line perfectly straight.)

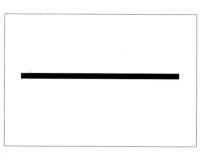

Step 2
From the menu, select Stroke and then select a broader stroke from the weight section in the menu (you also find options for cap and stroke styles here). This line has a rounded cap with a rounded join; "cap" refers to the shape of the end of the line, which may be rounded, straight, or oblique. It also applies to the type of join.

Step 3
Holding alt while you drag the line will duplicate the line you have drawn much faster than copying and pasting. Duplicate the shape and add a 90° horizontal line to get an idea of the shape that will be made with a corner.

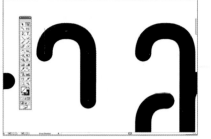

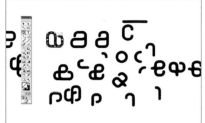

Step 4

Draw a circle using the Shape Tool (in the tool bar on the left). Use the white arrow to select certain points or anchors to delete; this will leave you with a quarter of a circle, creating a nice clean curve that you can add to.

Step 5

Place combinations of corners, curves, and vertical and horizontal lines upon one another to create random combinations of letterforms. You can adjust curves by pulling on the handles extended from the anchor.

Step 6

Look for shapes that contain the most resemblance to that of a familiar form, such as lowercase "a." Once identified, isolate that shape and paste it into a new document.

Step 7

Create the other letters from this shape. Start with an ascender; for "b" simply extend a stem from the top of the "a." From this develop other characters, e.g. reflect it (Object > Transform > Reflect) to get a "d" and flip it for a "p" and a "q." Remove the lower part of the "b" to get "h," then remove the stem for "n." Duplicate (hold alt and drag) the "n" and put them together for "m," and so on.

Step 8

To enhance legibility, ensure that all the ascenders and descenders are the same height and depth by using the guides available from the rulers at the top and left-hand side of the document window.

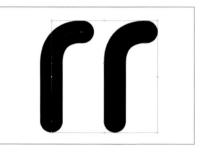

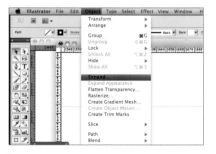

Step 9

Remove as many of the anchors and points as possible to create a smooth, solid letterform. Remove only unnecessary anchors. Use the white arrow tool to select points.

Step 10

Select a single letter and expand it by selecting Object > Expand.

Step 11

This turns the singular line into a multiple anchored shape, allowing you to make finer adjustments to joins and curves, among other things.

PROFILE Studio Dtam-TM

Halifax, UK

Paul Heys, a senior lecturer in Communication Design (BA Hons) at the University of Huddersfield in England, founded Studio Dtam-TM to supply the demand for CD, vinyl, and poster design for the underground music scene in Leeds. Since then the designers at Dtam-TM have created work for a number of UK labels and worked with international labels in Europe, Asia, Scandinavia, and North America. "Initially, when I began work as a designer, I was creating CD and vinyl covers for international punk bands in the late 1990s," explains Heys.

"The studio was officially founded a few years later and today we still work for many clients in the music industry. We design product with an importance on design for print." Heys tends to create most of his work digitally, particularly his lettering and type. "Ultimately I seem to end up working on my Mac but I'm open to any medium to get the job done in the right way," he explains. "A hybrid of new and old technology, an open mind, and a sense of adventure is how I like to work. Investing time and creativity in something that other people can use and appreciate, very much inspires my design."

▼ *Logo*
Dtam
To create the lettering for this logo, Heys drew the type freehand with the Pen Tool in Adobe Illustrator CS4, using a drawn arch as a reference.

► *Poster*
THE SIX HILLS
Heys added digitally
drawn elements to an
exciting type in order
to create the final
type for this poster.
Six Hills is considered
a cursed area outside
London, so the idea
with the design of
the poster was to
reference horror
and witchcraft.

TUTORIAL Studio Dtam-TM

Halifax, UK

This display type, by Paul Heys, was created for use on a poster that explored how mythical creatures are embedded in cultures and folklore. The poster was exhibited at the Daegu International Poster Exhibition in Korea in 2008. "This tutorial gives a basic introduction to type manipulation and designing your own display typeface," Hayes explains. "My rationale is that this is a gentle intro to bespoke type generation. Using an existing typeface helps in understanding how a font is created, and with a little work can be manipulated to create something fresh and original. Using this technique can also help in the realization of how building an original typeface from scratch is a labor-intensive operation and, in most cases, a notable and skilled profession."

INGREDIENTS

• A typeface
• Adobe Illustrator CS4

Step 1
Start by finding a basic typeface to work with, nothing too fancy, something that is easily editable; the simpler the better. Leave plenty of space between each glyph/character, as this will help with the editing process later.

◄ I AM LEGION

Step 2
To get full control and assign further editing options to each glyph, turn the "typed" glyphs into shapes or "outlines." By doing this you can now control the editing process. The area around the gylph after this stage is now referred to as a path.

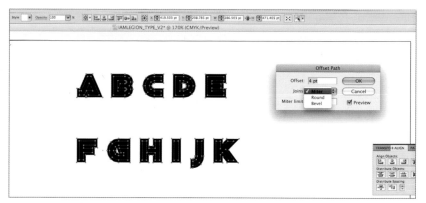

Step 3

Edit and expand the path, and make it bigger than its original. Use the Offset Path Tool for this, found in Object > Path.

Step 4

This is where the true feel of experimentation starts. The best way to experience the potential and limitations of this tool, like any software application tool, is to play around with the settings. Here an Offset 4pt is used (−4 would contract the path) Select the Joins option and set the Miter Limit to 4, to give a clean edge. Make sure the Preview button is selected to see the editing process in real time. Once complete, click OK.

Step 5

You now have a chunkier, customized example of the original typeface. The next step is to fine-tune the display type.

Step 6

Switch the view to Outline. The original path is still visible. This should be removed so as not to cause any editing problems in the future.

Step 7

Select the Add icon in the Pathfinder menu to remove the original outline and leave a solid shape.

Step 8

Make sure the style of each glyph works and sits together. This takes time, as this stage will really make your new typeface stand out. Some glyphs will always need more work than others. The more time spent on this stage, the stronger your typeface will be.

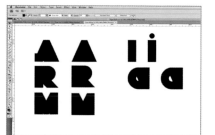

PROFILE Jason Grube

Seattle, USA

Grube will, by his own admission, use anything in front of him to create his unique, handcrafted lettering and type. "I am always trying out new materials. In my sketchbooks I work in pencil, pen, marker, watercolor pencils, acrylic, gouache, collage, and my current favorite, Sakura Gelly Roll pens," he explains. "I spend a lot of time thinking about, playing with, and sketching out different ideas before I arrive at a final design," he adds.

Grube trained at the University of Wisconsin and worked as an in-house designer before becoming freelance. He now works with both large and small clients, specializing in branding, illustration, and art direction. "As a designer I love solving problems using reason, creativity, and beauty. Type is interesting to me because letters are like little sculptures that humans give sounds and meanings to," explains Grube. "They are essentially meaningless shapes that allow us to record and communicate ideas, and I really enjoy manipulating these shapes and discovering how their meanings are affected."

For the majority of his projects Grube begins by drawing his letters and type in his sketchbook before finishing them off on his Mac using Adobe Illustrator for vector editing and a combination of drawing directly with a mouse and/or on a tablet. "Illustrator is great because it allows you to plot individual anchor points within your hand-drawn type and control the shape of the path using the Bézier control handles," explains Grube. "Creating a vector image in this way gives you something that is infinitely scalable: it exists as a formula rather than a set number of pixels."

◄ *Poster*
HOPE WITHOUT COMPLACENCY
Grube created this poster using a pencil, eraser, and Sakura Gelly Roll pen, before finishing it off in Adobe Photoshop.

▲ *Illustration*
A RUT IS ALSO A GROOVE.
This personal project was created using a pencil, eraser, pen, and Prismacolor marker.

▼ *Illustration*
GET OUT
This type, based on the font Daxline Pro Black, was created for Johnson Outdoors using Adobe Illustrator.

► *Greeting card*
MERRY CHRISTMAS
2009 HAPPY NEW
YEAR 2010
Grube drew this
poster by hand using
a Prismacolor marker.

TUTORIAL Jason Grube

Seattle, USA

◄ MOLASSES TREE

molassestree

Molasses Tree, a handmade children's clothing and fabric company, commissioned Jason Grube to create a logo for the company that captured the personality of the brand and would work not only on headed business paper, but could also be easily stitched onto clothing. It also needed to strike a balance between cute and professional. Inspired by molasses, leaves, thread, and sewing, the concept behind the design is the use of a single piece of "thread" to create the words Molasses Tree.

INGREDIENTS

- Pencil or pen
- Eraser
- Sketchbook
- Tracing paper
- Scanner
- Vector editing program

Step 1
Begin by sketching out some different ideas, experimenting with shape and form, and exploring different styles of lettering.

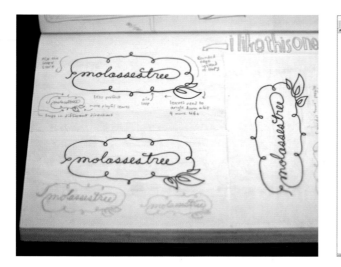

Step 2

Once you have found a style that you are happy with, focus the idea into a single concept and refine it until you have the final piece.

Step 3

Scan and import your drawing into the vector editing program.

Step 4

Using the mouse or drawing tablet, manually trace the letters and refine the shapes in your design.

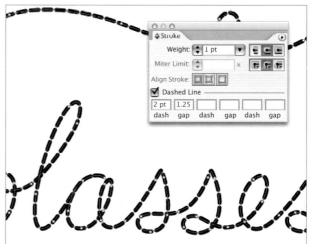

Step 5

Adjust the stroke weight and height of your letters and pattern, then add color to your design, if you so wish.

CHARACTER CREATION *Digitally Drawn*

GALLERY

▲ *Type specimen, Alex Varanese, Campbell, CA, USA*
I DON'T MIND BEING TRASH MINDED AS LONG AS YOU ARE TOO / Alphabet
Elektrotrash was constructed using individual sketches of geometrically versatile artifacts. Each element was modeled in 3D to create "kit parts" that could then be arranged in order to create letters. "Once the alphabet was done, I was able to form typographical layouts by simply arranging and duplicating the letters as necessary," explains Varanese. "By keeping everything in 3D until the last step, I could play with lighting, shadows, and perspective consistently across the entire piece, from a single letter to entire paragraphs."

▲ *Illustration, Jessica Hische, Brooklyn, USA*
SAY IT WITH FLOWERS
This decorative type was digitally hand-drawn, using the Pen Tool in Adobe Illustrator.

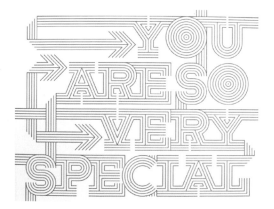

▲ *Illustration, Enormous Champion, Brooklyn, USA*
YOU ARE SO VERY SPECIAL
The lines and curves of this digitally drawn typeface were created in Adobe Illustrator using a rigid grid. The idea was to create the effect of a typographic maze. The quote is a lyric from a Radiohead song.

▲ *Posters, Rob and Barry van Dijck at Stay Nice, Breda, the Netherlands*
NATURAL / SMILE
The letters for these two posters were hand-drawn in Adobe Illustrator. They formed part of the *Don't Believe The Type* exhibition at the Ship of Fools gallery in The Hague.

◄ *Illustration, Jessica Hische, Brooklyn, USA*
PAY TO PLAY
This lettering was created for the *New York Times Magazine* by scanning a number of different coins and using Adobe Photoshop to create the composition.

▲ *Giftwrap, Jessica Hische, Brooklyn, USA*
HAPPY EVERYTHING
Created by hand in Adobe Illustrator, using the Pen Tool, this ribbon type was used on wrapping paper to convey the idea that the paper could be used for any occasion.

► *Illustration, André Beato, Lisbon, Portugal*
LISBON LOVERS
This lettering was inspired by the spirit of the city of Lisbon. Beato sketched the idea before drawing it again in FreeHand MX and finishing it in Photoshop.

◄ *Poster, Ian Bilbey (Represented by Central Illustration Association), Suffolk, UK*
LOVE
This lettering, for Paul Smith, was first shaped in wool before being photographed, imported into Adobe Photoshop, colored, and cleaned up ready for use.

CHARACTER CREATION *Digitally Drawn*

GALLERY

◄ *Posters, Rob and Barry van Dijck at Stay Nice, Breda, the Netherlands*
A GOOD DEED DOESN'T HURT / KNOT IN YOUR EARS
These two posters were commissioned by the Dutch primary school "De Rotonde" as part of a series spelling out the rules of the school. Type for the posters was first sketched by hand and then drawn in Adobe illustrator.

▲ *Illustration, Craig Redman at Rinzen, Australia/USA/Germany*
MORE SLEEP PLEASE
As the name suggests, this was inspired by sleep deprivation. It was created using FreeHand and Adobe Photoshop.

▶ *Illustration, Alex Varanese, Campbell, CA, USA*
POISON
Poison was created by Varanese using papercuts to create shadows, which in turn form the lettering. He used Autodesk 3ds Max to build the letters and Adobe Photoshop to composite the rendered image with color processing, texture, and other effects to achieve the desired tone.

▶ *Illustration, Alex Varanese, Campbell, CA, USA*
FIX ME OR DESTROY ME
The creation of Fix Me or Destroy Me was very much an organic process. Working in Autodesk 3ds Max, Varanese shaped and made each letterform as he worked his way through. Once completed, some modifications were necessary to tie it all together, but the overall shape and layout is the product of pure improvisation.

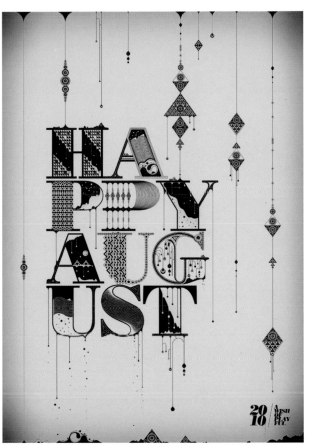

▲ *Poster, Karl Maier at Rinzen, Australia/ USA/Germany*
Lᴏsᴛ & ꜰᴏᴜɴᴅ
This type was created for Tourism Victoria, using individual elements that were digitally drawn by hand, while the final composition was created using FreeHand MX.

▶ *Calendar, Plenty, Buenos Aires, Argentina*
Hᴀᴘᴘʏ Aᴜɢᴜsᴛ
The lettering for this print began as a sketch before being fully hand-drawn in Adobe Illustrator. The design was inspired by the rainy, cold weather experienced in Argentina in August.

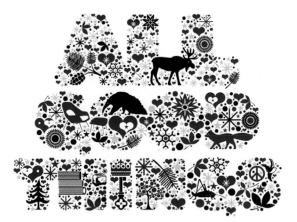

▲ *Illustration, Jessica Hische, Brooklyn, USA*
Lᴏᴠᴇ ʏᴏᴜʀ ʜᴇᴀʀᴛ
Inspired by the heart organ, this type was created for an article about women's health in *Chatelaine* magazine.

▲ *Illustration, Enormous Champion, Brooklyn, USA*
Aʟʟ ɢᴏᴏᴅ ᴛʜɪɴɢs
Using Adobe Illustrator, outline letters were drawn, populated with imagery, and then colored.

Chapter 4:

3D / Installation

The work shown on the following pages is the most obviously experimental of all the work in this book. With designers breaking away from the relatively restrictive 2D and exploring the new world of 3D, there are some great examples of designers and creatives thinking outside the box when it comes to creating lettering and type. Numerous methods and media are employed. For example, designer Vladimir Končar of Zagreb-based Studio Revolution has created lettering and type using materials such as beer caps, cacti, and beans, as can be seen on pages 112–113. London-based Amandine Alessandra created an entire alphabet using people, therefore allowing the type to move as and when was needed (see page 109). There are works on the following pages made using salt, grass, sugar cubes, ribbon, and ice. Together they provide inspiration as to how to create words using unusual materials and objects.

PROFILE Amandine Alessandra

London, UK

Alessandra hails from France but is based in London, where she studied at the London College of Communication and has now set up her own studio. Her practice, as a designer, is to draw on relationships between a place and a statement through handmade typography. Creating installation-based typography puts these two loves of hers together. She is also passionate about finding alternatives to print and computer-based communication, and enjoys working out alternative solutions to displaying messages in different environments.

"In order to allow myself to think in three, sometimes four dimensions, I tend to stay away from the computer in the first stage of a project, as it can limit creativity, given that we all use the same software and tools," she explains.

◄ *Poster*
Alphabet
Alessandra's Body Type alphabet is an experiment with the potential organic letterforms that emerge when reframing the body. It was inspired by a black-and-white image of a couple lying in a bed, their legs entangled, and then created using images of legs that Alessandra photographed.

◄ ▼ *Installation*
A SHUT BOOK IS JUST A BLOCK
This type is an experiment based on a quote by Thomas Fuller, "A book that is shut is just a block." Alessandra used the bookshelves as the "grid" in which to create an alphabet using different books.

"Ideas usually come when I'm not officially working; when I'm on the bus, or walking, or trying to sleep. I'm usually inspired by anything that triggers daydreaming; puns or Freudian slips are good, and idioms are an endless source of inspiration. I am also inspired simply by playing with words and idea association, in general."

Once Alessandra has an idea, sketches follow. She likes to visit the location where the type will be installed, in order to study the environment around it. To create her type, she starts with a test installation in a different location from the desired one, so she can identify any potential problems or issues, and work out a solution. She then creates the type in the specified location. As a majority of Alessandra's type is installation-based and non-permanent, photography gives each of them a second life, allowing the type to be displayed even when it no longer exists.

▶ *Installation*
"Type should move." /
Z O R / Alphabet
This letterform, Wearable, uses the human as the medium, therefore allowing the type to move. Each "performer" is dressed in black, apart from long-sleeved, day-glow boleros, which enable them to create the desired letter.

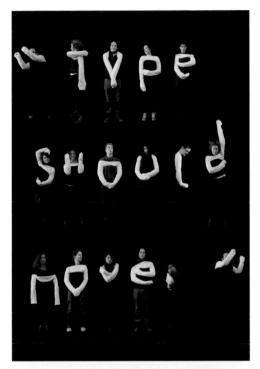

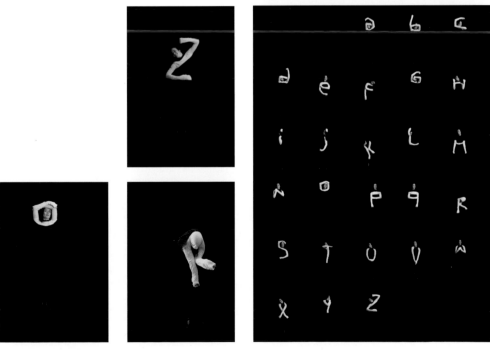

TUTORIAL Amandine Alessandra

London, UK

◄ ALWAYS

This work was created with the aim of looking at the ephemeral letterform—lettering that spells words, which become less and less relevant as they fade. Inspired by a winter in Canada, Alessandra became curious as to the side-effects of salt being used on snowy roads, and the wider implications of its use. To this end, she decided to create a word using salt on grass, and then monitored its evolution over a number of months. "I chose the word 'always' so as to exploit its double meaning: repetition and forever," she explains. "As the salt letters fade away, the grass surrounding it starts to die, burned by the sodium, leaving a well-defined scar in the green surface."

INGREDIENTS

- Stencil
- Protective film
- Cutting mat
- Craft knife
- Adhesive tape
- Salt
- Grass
- Time

Step 1

Print your chosen word out on a set of A4 (8⅛ x 11⅝in/297 x 420mm) sheets of paper; the bigger the better. Stick them together, and apply some protective film on to the whole thing, to prevent it from getting damp or damaged.

Step 2

Cut the letters out with a knife on a cutting mat. As you cut through the protective film and the paper, be sure to apply tape to the outline of each letter once cut, so as to secure the film and paper together.

Step 3

Time to move outside to your chosen location, where you will lay the stencil on the grass.

Step 4

Use a sieve to apply salt on to the stencil. Don't be afraid to put too much salt down, you must be able to see your word appear when you remove the paper. You could spray water on to it, to fix the salt and allow it to penetrate the soil.

Step 5

Remove the stencil to uncover the result. It is better if two people can do this, so as to prevent the paper from rubbing the grass. Take a photo.

Step 6

Wait a few weeks before revisiting the work and photograph it again.

Step 7

Again, wait a few more weeks and photograph it again. Repeat this twice more.

PROFILE Vladimir Končar

Zagreb, Croatia

Revolution is a design agency founded by Vladimir Končar, Gorjan Agačević, and Ozren Crnogorac. As a studio they combine graphic design with web design and development, and interactive multi-media projects. Their clients are mainly in culture or natural history, enabling them to work on diverse and varied topics. Clients include the Ministry of Culture of Croatia, the Museum of Contemporary Art, the Zagreb Brewery, Five Minutes Ltd, and many more. Vladimir Končar is also the creator of many varied experimental type designs, as can be seen in this selection from an ongoing project titled Diary Type—a personal typographic diary that started as an experiment. The idea for the series grew out of notes and sketches that Končar made over some time and includes alphabets made from beans, toothpicks, cacti, beer caps, and candy. "I love typography and the details of it. It is a massive preoccupation of my professional, and spare, time," explains Končar. "When I make type I like to have complete creative freedom.

▲ *Illustration*
DRINKING MAKES ME HAPPY
Beer caps were used to create this type. Each letter was arranged and photographed separately before being imported into Photoshop, where the light levels were equaled and the backgrounds cleaned up.

▼ *Illustration*
TYPOGRAPHY HURTS
This type was created by taking apart a number of cactus plants and arranging them to make letters. The title is a reference not only to the sting of a cactus, but also to bad typography, which hurts the viewer visually.

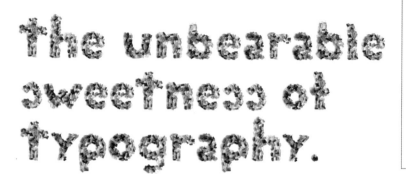

the unbearable sweetness of typography.

"I like to play with various objects I find, or that I have collected, and try to articulate the ideas that are inside my head." In the beginning Končar only created the letters he needed for a particular project, but now, as he says, he "obsessively creates whole alphabets." His ideas are inspired by many different things and often come to him when least expected. "I find inspiration everywhere around me, in films, exhibitions, concerts, plays, and just from hanging out with my friends. The best ideas somehow pop up unexpectedly in conversations or when you are just walking down a street."

▲ *Illustration*
THE UNBEARABLE SWEETNESS OF TYPOGRAPHY.
This type creatively bonds Končar's two loves: Gummy Bears and typography. Created by hand, it was photographed and Photoshopped, to lighten and clean it up.

▲ *Illustration*
Alphabet
Končar's leaf type, inspired by a morning walk, was created from birch tree leaves.

► *Illustration*
PICKING TEETH IS EASIER THAN PICKING THE RIGHT TYPE.
Thousands of toothpicks went into the making of these letters. Each letter was carefully laid out by hand and then photographed. The letters where then arranged into a sentence using Photoshop.

PICKING TEETH IS EASIER THAN PICKING THE RIGHT TYPE.

◀ Hello

This is Vladimir Končar's Beans type, which is part of his ongoing and ever-growing type project Diary Type. Made entirely of beans it is quite a time-consuming project but the results are good and of course you could use lots of different types of materials, other than beans. The main thing is to decide what type of letters you wish to make: sans serif, serif, slab, handwritten, freestyle, and so on. Once you have decided, then you are ready to begin.

INGREDIENTS

- Felt pen
- Drawing book
- Beans, 1lb (500g)
- Stable surface
- Camera and stand
- Pencils
- Table lamps
- Adobe Photoshop
- Checklist of letters
- Adobe Illustrator or InDesign

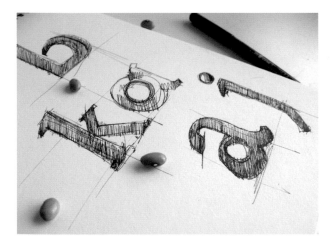

Step 1
Decide which kind of type to use, then sketch out the letters in which you will place the beans.

Step 2
Decide what surface you prefer to work on—white seems to be best. Place the beans carefully within your sketched letter. In the meantime make sure the camera is set up on a stand, ready to use.

Step 3
Mark out the necessary guidelines—baseline, mean line, capital height, height, and width of the letters.

Step 4
Level the beans, using pencils to ensure you get straight lines.

Step 5
Photograph each letter from several different positions in order to avoid the need to reshoot. Ideally connect the camera to a laptop, so that you can check that the image is good and usable.

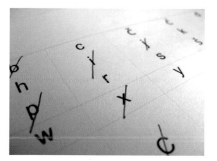

Step 6
On a prepared table, mark off the letters you've made to ensure that you don't miss any.

Step 7
Open each letter in Photoshop. Adjust the contrast, color, and sharpness if necessary.

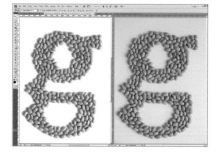

Step 8
You now have two options: wipe the background and save the letters as transparent PNGs, or leave the background, clean up any dust and dirt, and save them as JPEGs.

Step 9
Insert the letters into Illustrator or InDesign and make a grid with guides for the letter schedule. Then align them next to each other according to that grid. Manage the sizes of letters so that the set is as equable as possible. Your prepared letters are now ready to use.

PROFILE Me Studio
Amsterdam, the Netherlands

Me Studio is a small, independent design studio originally set up by two designers (Martin and Erik; hence the name "Me"). It is now a solo operation run by Martin Pyper. Although Pyper is the only one who sits in the office each day, Me Studio is made up of a network of designers and creatives who work on projects with Pyper on an ad hoc basis. "I always wanted to be a designer, I was lucky in that I knew that from a young age," explains Pyper. "I worked for quite a few different design and ad agencies for twenty years before setting up Me, just over five years ago." The studio currently works with a variety of different clients with a heavy skew toward cultural and not-for-profit organizations, including the Dutch National Ballet, and a number of theater and comedy club groups. In addition clients include photographers and other such creatives and the odd large corporate client. "What I really love about being a designer is that it allows me to meet such a great variety of people and to learn so much, and of course I love creating typefaces," he adds. "Typefaces are to me what food is to a chef."

▲ ▶ *Letter displays*
MEER / A B C
Various Dutch cheeses and a number of cookie cutters were used to create this cheese type. "I used a lot of cheeses before I found the right technique," Pyper explains.

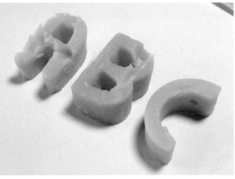

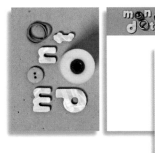

◀ *Letterheads and business cards*
MONODOT
Monodot, a film production company, commissioned Me Studio to create an identity with "lots of character." The basic font used is a found, photographed font painted white, and the O's were created using a variety of objects.

Pyper tends to begin all his projects by hand, sketching, drawing, and creating, although the computer does come into play later on in the design process. His interesting choice of materials and experimental nature make for some great design, as can be seen over the following pages.

► *Letterheads and business cards*
HELLO / ENJOY
Suiker Depot translates to Sugar Depot and as such was the inspiration behind the type and identity design for this Dutch film production company. Pyper created the letters using sugar cubes laid out on newsprint. These were then applied to various different printed company elements.

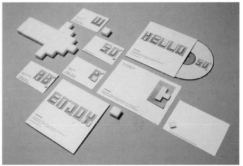

◄ ▼ *Letterheads and business cards*
WE / JANE
This type was created using ribbons, which were carefully folded by hand to create the required letters before being photographed ready for use on business cards and other printed matter.

Singel 120, 1015 AE Amsterdam, www.wejane.com

Wendy Hesseling
+31(0) 646426443 / wendy@wejane.com

we jane generates insights, ideas and concepts from a feminine perspective

TUTORIAL Me Studio

Amsterdam, the Netherlands

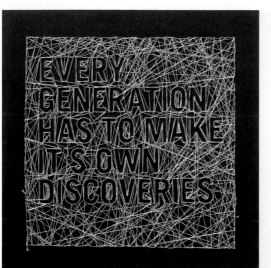 

Intended for use as a magazine spread illustration, the idea with this project was to create a typographic piece using one long piece of string and metal pins. It was inspired by a quote from Milton Glaser in the book *Looking Closer*; "Every generation has to make its own discoveries, even if they are old discoveries." "I find this a very liberating quote so used it as the starting point and inspiration for the design," explains Pyper. "Other than that the whole thing was worked out 'on the fly.' I made decisions on how to work on this as I progressed with it, that was the whole idea. It means that the technique, process, and content of the finished piece all relate to one another." The type was made using one continuous 328ft (100m) piece of string and an unspecified number of pins.

INGREDIENTS

- Printout of words
- Craft knife
- Steel sewing pins, 1000s
- Foam board, 2 pieces, c. ½in (5–10mm)
- White kite string, 328ft/ 100m
- Black wool, 2 small balls

Step 1

Begin by testing the letter size. First, print out the letters you require to use as a guide (Trade Gothic has been used here). Cut them out using a craft knife, place the guide on the foam board, and then place the pins in the corners and along the edges of your letter guides, so as to create frames for each letter.

Step 2
Start to loosely wrap the string around the pins, so you can see if you have the right size; if you don't, then reprint and retest.

Step 3
Once you have decided on the correct size, start to carefully place the pins into place and wrap the string around the pin frames. When you have finished each letter or word, remove the paper guide by cutting it out from underneath. Continue until you have completed all the letters.

Step 4
You can now start to wrap the pins in the string. For these words use the white string to fill the negative space in the layout, creating the letters from the black background. Start by filling in along the contours of the letters, as when drawing a letter in pen: first make the outline, then fill in the rest.

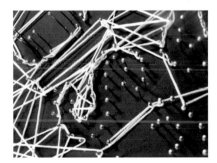

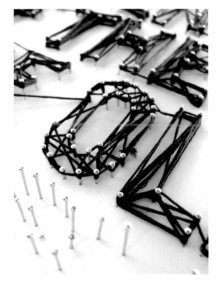

Step 5
You don't have to follow a strict pattern, i.e. each letter and word, one after the other. Instead you can chose a random and erratic path, stopping halfway through one letter, starting a different one, and then coming back to the other one later.

Step 6
Continue until you have completed all letters and words. Remember the aim is not to cut the string but instead to use one continuous piece.

TIP
Carefully judge the size you make the original piece compared with the final reproduction size—if you make it too big, the handmade feel will disappear. This is because, if it is reduced down too much in print, it could end up looking too perfect, which would defeat the idea of making it by hand.

Step 7
Start on the other page using the black wool. This time you will be using the wool to fill in and create the letters, so you need to move from one letter to the next.

PROFILE FromKeetra

Baltimore, USA

FromKeetra is the name under which Keetra Dean Dixon works. She developed many of her core design and artistic objectives during her masters studies at the Cranbrook Academy of Art. Since then her work has gained notoriety for its friendly nature and its often heightened emotional nature. It has also gained her a presidential award, a place in the permanent design collection at the SFMOMA, and the honorable ranking of ADC Young Gun.

▲▼ *3D lettering*
SENSITIVE
This lettering was created using die forms made to fit a custom extrusion system. Clay was then pressed through the die, allowing for the squirmy letters to find their path.

She now runs a studio out of Baltimore, as well as leading courses as an Associate Professor at the Maryland Institute College of Art. Having started in general graphic design, branding, and ephemera, she often collaborates with the LAB at Rockwell Group and, in addition, is commissioned to create a large amount of self-authored work. Watch brand Swatch asked her to create a treatment for a design event addressing the topic of "meeting new people." Much of her work relies heavily on typographic messaging partnered with material studies, as an investigation into the fallibility of communication, understanding, and intention. Inspired by "almost everything" she says, "What I love about being a designer and creating lettering and type is getting lost in the details and lovely minutiae."

▲ *Decorative piece*
THROUGHOUT
Positive type forms were created and then hand-dipped in wax of varying colors. The object was then sliced open and the positive type form extracted to create the final piece.

TUTORIAL FromKeetra

Baltimore, USA

Keetra Dean Dixon is FromKeetra. This self-authored project was created to convey a sense of wonder. "The idea behind the creation of this piece of work was to create something that appeared full of effortlessness and wonder," Dixon explains. "It was inspired by the feeling of elation and by what one can create with found ephemera." This has been achieved by using old envelopes, prints, and maps to create the letters and then a clever use of photography to create the illusion of the letters standing up on their own. As Dixon explains: "You will need a patient model for this project, as positioning the letters and then capturing a crisp image takes some time."

► WONDER

INGREDIENTS

- Selection of interesting found paper (e.g. double-sided prints, envelopes, maps)
- Ruler
- Craft knife
- Thread
- Superglue
- Camera
- Adobe Photoshop

Step 1
Deconsruct all the material you have, in this instance an envelope, and prepare them for cutting.

Step 2
Next, take your craft knife and ruler, and carefully trim strips off your paper, approximately ¼in (5mm) wide.

Step 3

Take the thin strip of paper and carefully fold and curl in order to form the desired letter.

Step 4

If there is too much paper, or you want to create a slightly different shape, trim unwanted or excess paper away.

Step 5

Refine your final letterform by softly curling segments of it by holding the paper between finger and thumbnail, and gently pulling the paper across your thumbnail.

Step 6

Cut a 5in (12.5cm) piece of thread. Tie a small, ring-sized loop in one end of it and then carefully glue the other to your letterform. Try to place the thread at a central point of the letterform, so that it will hang at a level angle in your final piece.

Step 7

Slip the hooped end of the thread over your model's finger, so as to suspend the letter. Set up your camera and lighting to photograph the letter.

Step 8

Import the photograph into Photoshop and flip 180°. Repeat to create all the different letters using different papers and then import into Photoshop and piece together to create your final image.

TUTORIAL Bank

Berlin, Germany

◄ PNEUMA

Berlin-based Bank was founded by French/German duo Sebastian Bissinger and Laure Boer. Their idea for this project was to experiment and use something unusual to create a series of letters. They decided to try using the inner tube of a bicycle tire.

"We were interested in finding out if we could create all the letters of the alphabet, as well as full stops, commas, etc," explains Bissinger. "We wanted to turn work into fun. We always try to keep this energy, whether working on personal or client projects."

INGREDIENTS

- Bicycle tire
- Pin
- Bicycle repair kit
- Bicycle pump
- Camera
- Adobe Illustrator

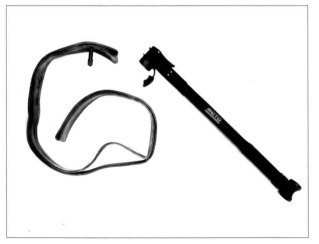

Step 1
Using a pin, pierce the tire and inner tube. Remove the flat inner tube from within the tire.

Step 2
Fix the hole in the inner tube and then pump it back up, so that it's ready for you to start creating your letters.

 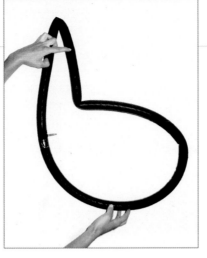 

Step 3

Create letters by shaping the inner tube with your hands. Once you are happy with your letter, photograph it, and then move on to the next one.

TIP

Set your camera and lighting up in one place and shoot all your letters from there to ensure continuity with light and distance.

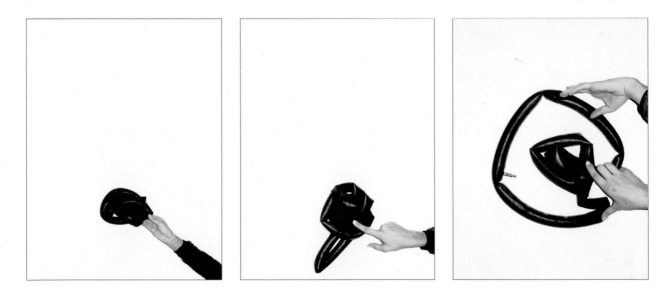

Step 4

When you have completed all the letters of the alphabet; start to work on the punctuation and other symbols, such as the @ sign, before importing your images into Illustrator to lay out as you desire.

GALLERY

◄ Illustration, Lisa Rienermann, Berlin, Germany
HAPPY NEW YEAR
This German greeting was created using confetti. In addition, each step was photographed and later used to create an animation.

▲ Illustration, Alex Robbins, London, UK
KEEP ON THE GRASS
Created for *Ace* magazine's Wimbledon issue, this type was made using grass. Robbins sketched out the lettering, mowed his own lawn, and then used the cuttings to created the letters.

▲ ► Book cover, Handverk, Oslo, Norway
HOTEL BORG, NICOLA LECCA
The brief for this project was to create type for a book in which a musician was the central character. To this end, the designers at Handverk created type using crumpled sheet music.

◄ Invitation, Lisa Rienermann, Berlin, Germany
PARTY
The type for this housewarming invitation was created using towels, fruit, shoes, flowers, decorations, and confetti, all found in the apartment where the party was held.

▶ *Light paintings, Chris Rubino and Anthony Geernaert, New York, USA*
SECRETS / NEVER
Lengths of lights were used to create words and long exposures on the camera experimented with to create the final images.

▶ *Print, Toben, Sydney, Australia*
LOOKING FOR ROMANCE
The layout for the lettering on this print was created digitally and then printed to scale. Wire was then twisted, bent, and laid out as per the printed design. The barbed wire parts were added last, before it was all sprayed gold and photographed.

▲ *Illustration, Alex Robbins, London, UK*
TREAT YOUR FEET
This was created for the Lawn Tennis Association's magazine. Robbins marked out holes on orange card to create a grid for the desired letters, before threading laces through the holes to created the final piece.

▶ *Illustration, Lisa Rienermann, Berlin, Germany*
NOISE
This logotype was created for a group exhibition held at The White Salon in Berlin. The letters were constructed from hand-cut paper letters, which were then scanned into Photoshop and layered.

GALLERY

◀ **Poster, Thomas Forsyth, London, UK**
I'M SKINT BUT I STILL LOVE MY MUM
This Mother's Day message was created using a collection of random items found in Forsyth's home. He sketched a basic layout before piecing together the letters using the objects. It was then photographed and cleaned up in Adobe Photoshop.

▲▼ *Book cover, Handverk, Oslo, Norway*
THESIS ON THE EXISTENCE OF LOVE
A book cover made of books was the idea behind this type. Books were positioned to create letters, then photographed from above. The finished cover was created in Photoshop.

▲ *Installation, Ruiter Janssen, The Hague, the Netherlands*
NEW FOUND
This lettering was set up to visually represent Kosovo's independence from Serbia. The words were built from rubble at an old fabric factory in Skendraj, Drenica.

▲ *3D graphic, Toben, Sydney, Australia*
TOBEN
This lettering was created for design studio Toben. "Toben" stems from the German word for playing freely and this formed the starting point of the design. The letter "T" was created using a chandelier, "o" using sunglass lenses, "b" using fabric-covered foam balls on a wire, "e" using a cardboard cutout, and "n" using cut chopsticks.

◀ *Album cover, Christine Föllmer, Hamburg, Germany*
AMOS / SHOWTIME
The design of the lettering for this album cover was inspired by shoelaces. Föllmer sketched out a template for the text before creating holes, threading the laces, and then photographing them.

▲ *Alphabet, Andrew Lister,*
Norwich, UK
N
This string lettering was created as part
of an experimental typography workshop.
Pins and string have been used to create
the 3D letters, based on the font DIN.

▶ *Illustration, Raphaël Bastide,*
Montpellier, France
THE QUICK BROWN FOX JUMPS OVER THE
LAZY DOG
In this project, space and typography
are explored using different materials
and different techniques to spell out
this common pangram.

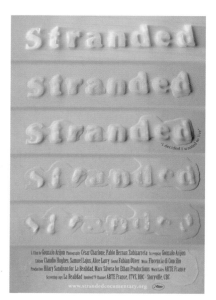

◀ *Installation, Ruiter Janssen,*
The Hague, the Netherlands
STRANDED
To create this ice lettering, Janssen
first cut the letters from wood, then
put them in a vacuum machine, which
pressed a heated plastic plate on to the
letters, before filling the shapes with
water and freezing them ready for
use on this poster.

▲ *Illustration, Hjärta Smärta,*
Stockholm, Sweden
BORIS
This typeface was created using
earrings. Starting with a few words,
it has since been developed into an
entire alphabet, with different weights.

CHARACTER CREATION *3D / Installation*

GALLERY

◄ ▲ *TV idents, Handverk, Oslo, Norway*
Copenhagen / Oslo / North
These are program titles and TV idents created for Norwegian television channel TV2. The program *The Road to Copenhagen* was about climate change, so this type was created using recycled materials, including milk cartons, milk crates, cardboard boxes, and glass jars, as well as people.

◄ ▲ *Installation, Raphaël Bastide, Montpellier, France*
New
Deep is a project that explores the idea of creating letters and words in white water. Bastide used black pearls to create the letters, which he weighted down using different lengths of transparent thread.

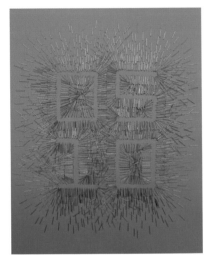

▲ *Illustration, Alex Robbins, London, UK*
05/10
This date was created for *Wired* magazine, using a stapler in such a way that the numbers were created out of the negative space.

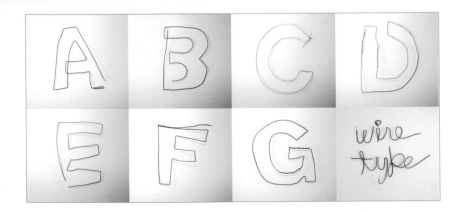

◄ *Alphabet, Rina Miele at Honey Design, Sleepy Hollow, USA*
A B C D E F G Wire Type
Miele used colored strips of telephone wire to create these letters, with Helvetica as a reference.

▲ *Illustrations, Ed Nacional, Brooklyn, USA*
I COULD USE A FEW MORE SHIRTS. / Alphabet
The type shown here was created using a selection of different ties to create each letter of the alphabet, in both upper and lower case.

▲ *Illustration, August Hefner, Brooklyn, USA*
SERM: SELECTIVE ESTROGEN RECEPTOR MODULATOR
SERM is a hormone therapy used to reduce the risk of breast cancer, so the lettering was created using pink ribbon (the universal symbol for breast cancer), double-sided tape, and sunlight, then edited in Photoshop.

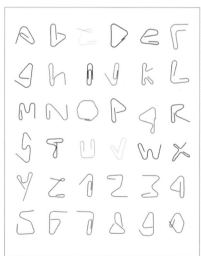

▲ *Installation, Raphaël Bastide, Montpellier, France*
HI.
This self-initiated project was created using salt, which has been brushed away to form the letters in the negative space.

▲ *Poster, Plenty, Buenos Aires, Argentina*
PLAY WITH SHAPES
The lettering for this poster was created using colored geometric shapes, laid out by hand on grass to form the letters.

▲ *Poster, Vladimir and Maksim Loginov at Hand Made Font, Tallinn, Estonia*
Alphabet
That everyday office item, a paper clip, was used to create this alphabet.

GALLERY

◀ ▲ *Signage, Andrew Byrom, Long Beach, USA*
OPEN / R
Byrom Temporary Signage System is a pop-up alphabet made from waterproof nylon wrapped around a fiberglass pole frame. The letters can be collapsed using an elastic cord running inside the pole, allowing them to be transported.

◀ *Illustration, Daryl Tanghe, Seattle, USA*
BLOOM / GLOOM
This typeface is based on seasonal depression. Flowering plants were used to construct Bloom, the summer variation of the typeface. For the winter version, Gloom, the Bloom lettering was laid out on light-sensitive paper under bright light to create a faded, semi-transparent version of Bloom, alluding to the feelings people who suffer with seasonal depression experience.

▲ *Flyer, Plenty, Buenos Aires, Argentina*
JUNE 5, THE OVNIS, LA FIESTA WALDORF @ BELUSHI HONDURAS
All elements of this flyer were created using Play-Doh on a sheet of acrylic.

▲ *Wall hanging, Daryl Tanghe, Seattle, USA*
GUT
This piece of type started as a drawing before being sawn out of a piece of wood, which was then stained and displayed on a wall.

▲ *Display piece, Vladimir and Maksim Loginov at Hand Made Font, Tallinn, Estonia*
Alphabet
This alphabet was created using string, which has been shaped and knotted to form each letter.

▲ *Poster, Christine Föllmer, Hamburg, Germany*
FESTIVAL OF YOUNG TALENT
This poster was designed for a German art festival. Föllmer wove strips of red and white plastic in such a way as to create the desired words.

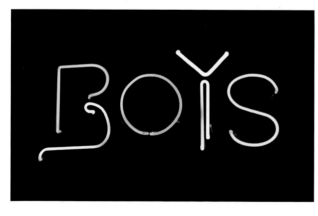

▲ *Light painting, Hjärta Smärta, Stockholm, Sweden*
BOYS
This lettering was created using recycled neon tubes. The idea was to make use of otherwise unwanted neon lights to create letters and words, which were then lit up and photographed in dark rooms.

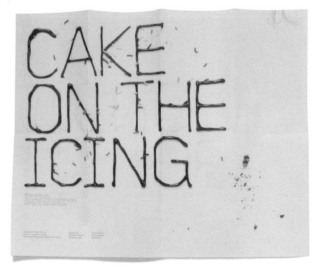

▲ *Poster, Underline Studio, Toronto, Canada*
CAKE ON THE ICING
The type created for this promotional poster for InterAccess Electronic Media Arts Centre, Toronto, has been crafted using icing. The letters were written out and then photographed.

Chapter 5:

Found or photographed

This chapter looks at letters and alphabets that designers and creatives have found within everyday objects in the surrounding environment. Often hidden and difficult to find, compiling such alphabets can take some time. Lisa Rienermann, whose work can be seen on pages 136–137, walked around the city of Barcelona for a number of days in order to complete her found alphabet. It was created using the sky in the space between the city buildings. Then there is Abba Richman, whose work can be seen on page 140. She took a number of months to complete her alphabet, which has been created using found objects in various cities around Israel. This chapter does not contain tutorials but rather detailed explanations as to how and why each of the featured designers and creatives developed their found type. There are some inspiring examples here of how looking hard and seeing beyond the obvious can result in found letters in many of the everyday objects surrounding us and in different spaces and places.

PROFILE Lisa Rienermann

Berlin, Germany

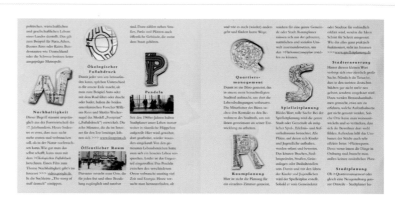

Lisa Rienermann is an animator and photographer. "I started my studies with photography as my major, but after two years I noticed that my approach to photography was very graphic, so I decided to change my major to graphic design because I thought of them as separate fields," she explains. "I now realize that they can be one thing and this is my main focus—to combine different parts of design; to make a picture typographic and make text with a picture. I love it when type becomes a picture and then also the other way around, you can read pictures." Inspired by the world around her, Rienermann takes a camera with her wherever she goes and is always looking for new images. She loves finding letters in things other people don't see, like letters in stains or a hole in the wall that looks like a face. "Discovering something is always a great moment, like when I had the locks changed in my workspace. I was standing there and I looked up and saw a face," she explains. "A part of the paint had come off and, together with the wall plugs, it looked like a little face to me." As well as found type Rienermann works with her hands creating type using found objects or cut-out paper, as well as painting letters. "Of course sometimes creating lettering or type in this way is more time-consuming but I really like the handmade warmth that lettering or type, created by hand, gives to a finished project," she explains. "You can see the difference that it makes." Rienermann works for a variety of different clients, including cultural institutions, publishers, advertising agencies, and fellow designers.

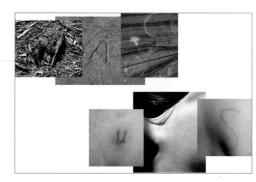

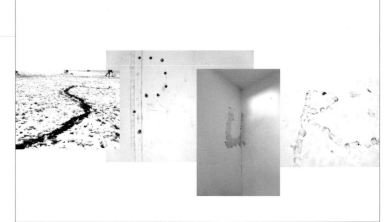

◄ *Illustration*
Alphabet

This type was created for the publisher Beltz & Gelbery for use in a children's book about discovering cities, *Entdecke deine Stadt*. The idea was to create a dictionary-style layout and design for the book. To this end Rienermann wanted to create each letter of the alphabet in a way that would appeal to 10-year-olds and also relate to the idea of the city. She spent many hours studying maps of cities looking for roads that crossed or bent in such a way as to create letters or shapes. Once she had found each letter, she scanned the details from the maps and imported them into InDesign, where she created and saved each letter as an individual image. Rienermann then printed each letter, cut it out, and then layered more paper underneath before scanning it again and adding a drop shadow in InDesign to create the final map letter.

▲ *Letter images*
WASUNS/SPUR

The idea behind this project was the thought that even when things disappear, they leave traces. "I created different booklets, each of which looks at different aspects of traces," explains Rienermann. "Finding them, leaving them and analyzing them. As a lot of the trace letters can only be read if you put them in context, the title of the project can only be read when all four booklets are laid next to each other: 'Was uns bleibt ist nur die spur,' or 'What stays is only a trace.'" The letters were found on skin, in wood, on the footpath, after the rain, and more. After collecting all the letters Rienermann imported them into Photoshop, adjusted the colors, and then composed the words.

◄ *Letter images*
WILL YOU LOOK AT ME? / YEAH

"Standing in something like a little courtyard in Barcelona I looked up and saw houses, the sky, clouds, and the letter Q," explains Rienermann of how she began her Type in the Sky project. "The negative space between the houses formed the letter Q. I loved the idea of the sky as words, the negative being the positive, and decided that if I could find a Q, other letters should be somewhere around the corner." From here Rienermann spent many days walking around looking up at the sky for letters and bit by bit she found each letter of the alphabet. Once completed, the alphabet was used to create a booklet containing a folded poster. On unfolding the poster the words read "Will you look at me?" the idea being that the poster, or the sky, is asking the viewer this question. The answer comes when the last piece is unfolded to read, "Yeah."

PROFILE Karin von Ompteda

London, UK

Karin von Ompteda is a doctoral researcher at the Royal College of Art, London, and her work is specifically focused on integrating scientific and design approaches to the topic of typeface legibility, with particular interest in low-vision readers. As well as typeface legibility research she also runs a commercial typographic design practice specializing in found type, 3D constructed letterforms, such as rapid prototyping and laser cutting, and digital font design. However, it was her found-type projects that first got von Ompteda interested in the topic of typeface legibility. She was interested in exploring the limits of legibility within found-type projects. "When one engages in found-type projects, one invariably has to ask over and over again:

what is it about an 'a' that makes it an 'a,' and so on," she explains. "The designer is challenged to discern the features necessary for their audience to recognize a letter as the one intended… It's all about observation, one has to keep an open mind regarding how a letter should look if you are searching for it in an unconventional medium. I also do a lot of rotate/reflect/crop in my mind when I am on the hunt for a letter." Von Ompteda is inspired by the vast form differences that are possible for letters, in contrast to the striking similarity of letters across text typefaces. "This kind of work is invariably analytical and exceptionally satisfying, and for me was the first step toward pursuing academic typography research," she adds. "I also love knowing that I'm working with an ancient technology."

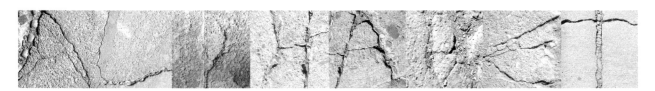

▲ *Letter images*
ALPHABET
Shown here are von Ompteda's found concrete letters. This project was conceived while she was walking home. "I had never realized that the streets were full of capital 'A's, designed by cracks in the concrete," she explains. "This led me to look for more letters until I found this set." The project was executed through photography and then cropping using Photoshop. Cropping played a critical role in the project, as many letters were not self-contained, with their cracks extending well down the road so in these cases cropping was necessary to complete the letters.

▼ *Letter images*
ALPHABET
"There is a moment in every designer's life when they start to see letters in everything, for instance a 't' in a slab of meat," explains von Ompteda. This grew into her Red Meat project. Von Ompteda examined meat at a number of butchers and bought cuts where the bones resembled letters. The final forms were created by removing flesh or bone, and each letter was photographed on a cutting board. She did not manipulate the images at all, simply processed and cropped them in Photoshop.

GALLERY

Frise et papier peint

Mathilde Nivet
2007
Tous droits réservés

▲ ► *Poster and catalog, Mathilde Nivet,*
Paris, France
PATCH BUILDING / Alphabet

This alphabet was created using found shapes
and existing structures within buildings around
the cities of London, Paris, and Berlin. The idea
of this self-initiated project was to focus on
photographing the more unattractive suburban
buildings that were built around the 1960s and
1970s, and then using found elements, as well
as manipulated elements, to create a complete
alphabet. It took Nivet a number of months to
collect the images of the different buildings.
As she traveled and walked around the three
different cities, she would have her Canon
Powershot A95 with her ready to use when she
spotted a suitable building. "I was very careful
in choosing the buildings that I wanted to shoot
for the collection," she explains. "I selected them
based on their shape and what letterform they
looked like or could work as." Once Nivet had
collected all the required images, she imported
them into Adobe Photoshop to adjust the levels,
manipulate some of them into the desired shape,
create shadows, and give them a 3D effect. This
then completed her building lettering.

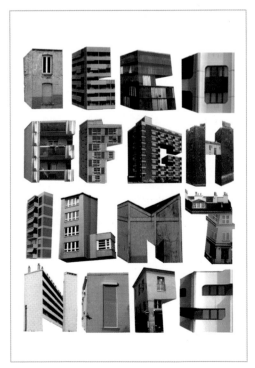

GALLERY

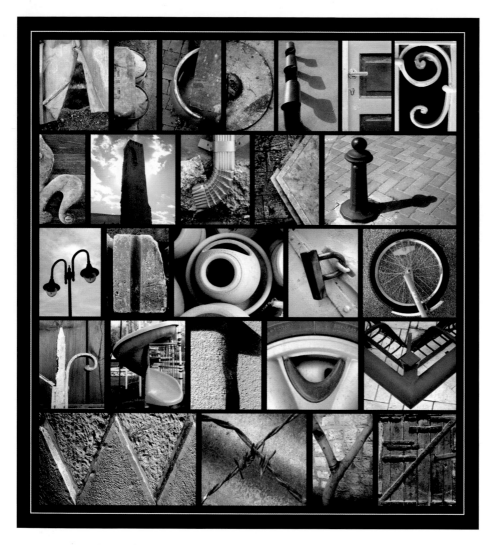

◄ *Poster, Abba Richman, Efrat, Israel*
Alphabet

Richman works as a designer and also teaches photography and design. This is her found alphabet project, completed over four months. Using her Nikon D200, Richman set out to find all the letters of the alphabet somewhere within the cities of Efrat, Jerusalem, and Tel Aviv, and then compiled them into a complete alphabet. "It was an interesting challenge for me," she explains. "The idea of finding letterforms within everyday objects or buildings really appealed to me. Some of the letters were actually quite easy to find, like the O, P, and D, but others were much more difficult, for instance the Q, S, and the Z. Those I had to look carefully for and really think about where I might find them around the cities I was photographing in." The montage has been published as a poster and studied by photography students, both in the UK, as part of the Photography A-level and Diploma of Photography syllabuses, and the USA, as part of the College of Fine Art Photography courses.

▶ *Poster, Erik Tabuchi,*
Paris, France
Alphabet

Here is an alphabet made up
of letters on the rear-end of
trucks. The images were taken
on the French highways over
the course of four years. Even
though each letter is different,
the idea was to make the
alphabet coherent.

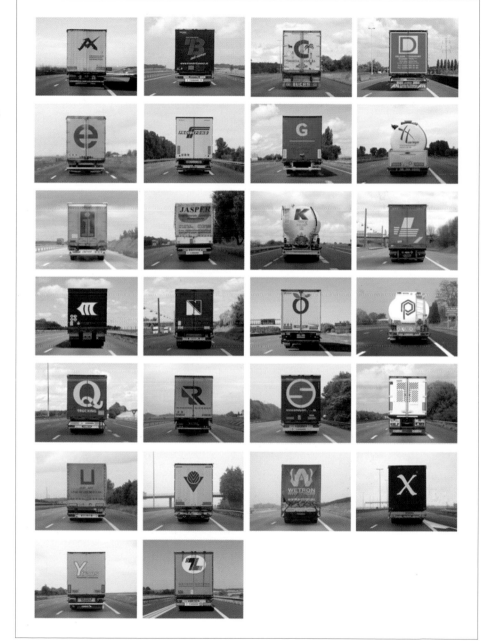

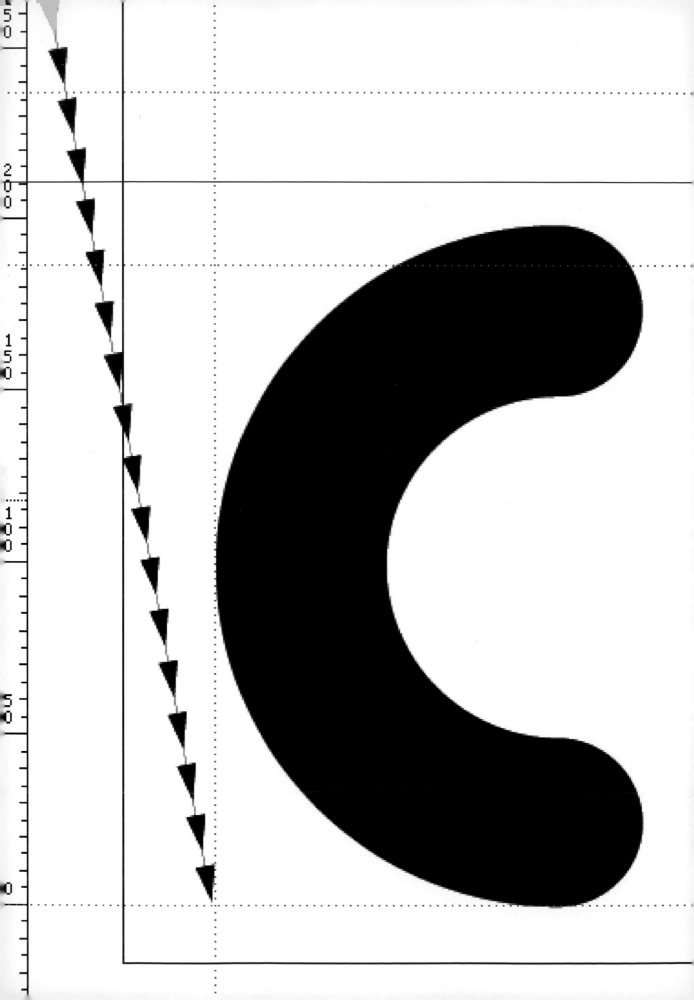

Font
creation

Chapter 6:

Preparing characters

Once a designer has created lettering or type, in order
for it to be usable by someone else it must be made into
a full working font. To do this, the letters or type must
be scanned or photographed, imported into a computer,
and then taken through a program such as FontLab
or Fontographer. This chapter guides you through the
steps required.

The anatomy of type

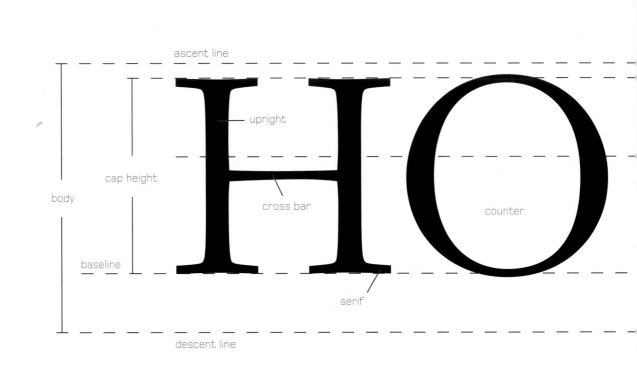

ascent line

upright

cap height

cross bar

body

counter

baseline

serif

descent line

Type formats

OpenType
This font format was developed to enable cross-platform use. It works on Mac OS 8.6, 9, X, Windows, and Linux. It supports OpenType layout features and allows more than 65,000 characters, including Unicode.

TrueType
PC TrueType is used mainly on Windows and other PC-based operating programs. TrueType fonts can provide good legibility at small point sizes. TrueType can be used as a cross-platform font on Mac OS 9 and later versions. TrueType format is also available for Mac OS as Mac TrueType.

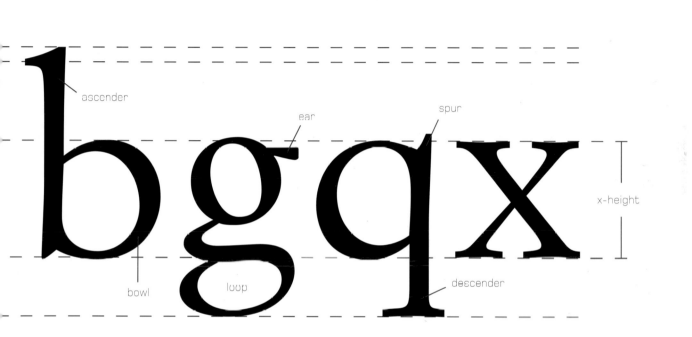

PostScript TypeOne

A font format mainly used in the Macintosh environment. The font consists of two parts: the suitcase, which contains the metrics and kerning information; and the printer font, which contains the font outlines. Both parts must be included in the fonts folder.

PostScript TypeThree

This type format, now obsolete, had the ability to print halftones and patterns.

From typeface to font

There is a tricky-to-explain, rarely understood, but key difference between a typeface and a font. "Typeface" refers to the design of the alphabet: the shape of the letters, numbers, and symbols that make up the design of a specific type. "Font" refers to the digital file that contains/describes a typeface. Think of the font as a little piece of software that tells the computer and printer how to display and print the typeface.

How do you take a typeface or set of characters and turn it into a font? There are a number of software packages that allow you to make fonts, the main two being FontLab and Fontographer, but before they can do their work, there are a number of preparatory stages that you must complete.

1. First, you need to create any missing letterforms and punctuation symbols—many fonts are let down by having inadequate punctuation, which renders them unusable. You could also think about creating some ligature pairs, but this is down to your preference and the style of font you are creating.

2. Next, make sure all your letterforms and punctuation marks contain only black and white, and remove any unwanted details or background.

3. Finally, you must convert your characters into vector illustrations. This can be done in Illustrator.

This chart shows the variety of paths you can take in order to turn your characters into a finished font, depending on your original character forms and on what software you prefer to use.

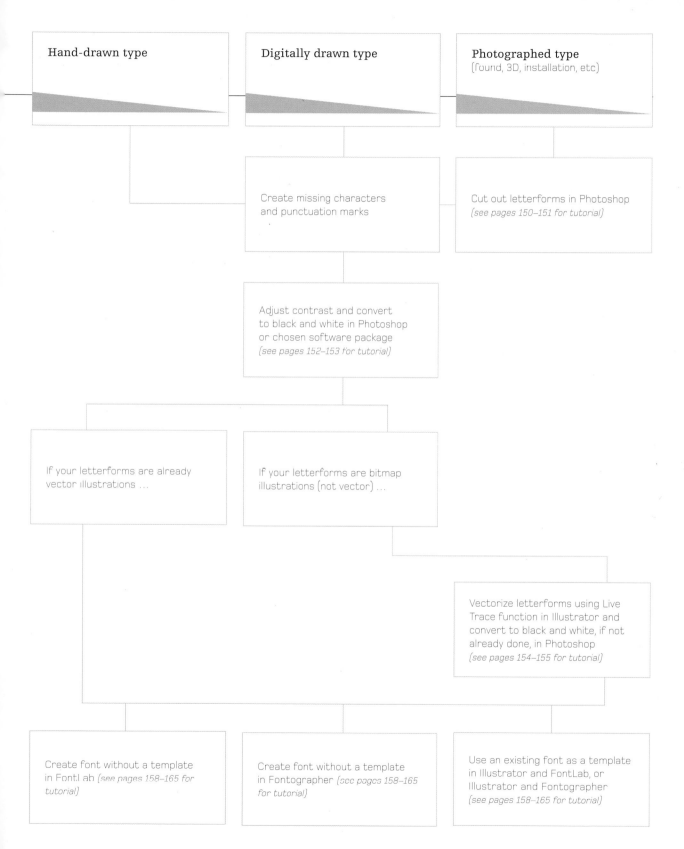

Hand-drawn type

Digitally drawn type

Photographed type
(found, 3D, installation, etc)

Create missing characters
and punctuation marks

Cut out letterforms in Photoshop
(see pages 150–151 for tutorial)

Adjust contrast and convert
to black and white in Photoshop
or chosen software package
(see pages 152–153 for tutorial)

If your letterforms are already
vector illustrations …

If your letterforms are bitmap
illustrations (not vector) …

Vectorize letterforms using Live
Trace function in Illustrator and
convert to black and white, if not
already done, in Photoshop
(see pages 154–155 for tutorial)

Create font without a template
in FontLab *(see pages 158–165 for
tutorial)*

Create font without a template
in Fontographer *(see pages 158–165
for tutorial)*

Use an existing font as a template
in Illustrator and FontLab, or
Illustrator and Fontographer
(see pages 158–165 for tutorial)

Extracting letterforms from photographs

If the characters you wish to turn into a font are in photographs, you will need to cut them from their background. This is true whether they are photographs that capture found letterforms, or created characters, like this "m" and "e" made from cheese. The easiest and most commonly used software for this is Photoshop.

▲ *Me Studio*
ME

Step 1
Open your photograph in Photoshop and draw an accurate path around each of your letterforms.

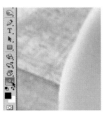

Step 2
Zoom into your image using the Zoom Tool located in your Tools panel (or the shortcut cmd + =) so that you can see your character edges clearly.

Step 3
Select the regular Pen Tool from the Tools panel (cmd + p). There are a number of pen tools, but the standard one draws with the greatest precision.

Step 4
Position your pen cursor on the edge of your letterform, then click and release once to place your first anchor point.

Step 5
Now click again farther along the path to position your second anchor point, but this time click and hold. Drag your cursor and you'll notice that the Pen Tool pointer changes to an arrowhead. This dragging action adjusts the curve of your lines between two anchor points. Once you are happy with the curve, release.

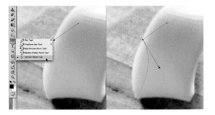

Step 6
If, after you've released your mouse button, you still aren't satisfied that the curve follows the edge of your letterform, you can adjust it with the Convert Point Tool located in your Tools panel (press alt while hovering over the end of one of your anchor point handles). Click and hold down on the end of an anchor point handle and you can drag it around to adjust the curve of the line. You can do this with any point, at any time.

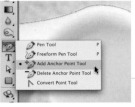 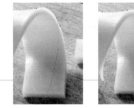 

Step 7

Space your anchor points so they follow a simple edge in your image that can be mirrored by a single line with a curve but no bends. If your anchor points are too far apart, you can add more in between using the Add Anchor Point Tool located in your Tool panel. Click and release on the path between the existing anchor points and drag this new point to a position off the edge of your letterform. You can change the angle of the joining lines using the Convert Point Tool. Continue creating a path around your letterform until you have returned to your first anchor point. Click on this to complete your path.

Step 8

If you have more than one letterform in an image, draw around each letterform individually. Make sure you also draw around any negative space in your letterforms.

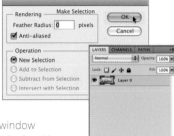

Step 9

Open your Paths panel to see your completed path. Go to the drop-down menu in the top right-hand corner of the panel, scroll down, and choose Make Selection.

Step 10

In the Make Selection window Anti-aliased will be checked as the default setting; leave this, make sure Feather Radius is set to 0 and that New Selection is checked, then click OK.

Step 11

Now that you have just your letterforms selected, you want to block out the background with a mask. You could just delete the background, but this would prevent you adjusting your path later; a mask is preferable because the image is retained, you just can't see it. Go back to your Layers panel and click on the Mask button at the bottom of the window. The background becomes hidden, and you'll see your mask appear in miniature next to your image in the Layers panel.

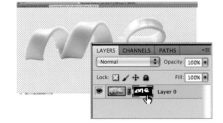

Step 12

If you now notice that you have cut off any parts of your letterforms, or included part of the background, you can adjust the mask. Making sure you have your mask selected and not your image, add white to the mask layer to expand it or black to remove it.

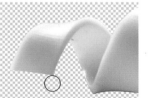 

Step 13

Once you are happy with your path and mask you should save your image as a JPEG file. You are now ready to turn it into a black-and-white image from which you can make a font (see pages 152–153 for tutorial).

Converting to black and white

A font cannot contain any color or shades of gray—only 100% black and what appears as white, but is actually negative space. Think about typing or designing with a font—the only way to change its color is to change the color of the text as a whole. Because of this, the next step in the process is to strip out all color and shading from your letterforms. You can do this in Photoshop (as described here) or in Illustrator, as part of the vectorization process (see pages 154–155 for tutorial), but working in Photoshop gives you more control over which colors and tones become black and which become white.

Step 1
This is not difficult to do if your letterforms are already one color only. Simply open your image in Photoshop and go to Image > Adjust > Black & White (or click on the Black & White button in the Adjustments panel).

Step 2
The Black and White window will appear. Leave the Preset on Custom and push all the sliders to the far left. Each color should now have a value of -200%. It is important to note that the black-and-white adjustments function only works if either the 8 Bits/Channel or 16 Bits/Channel and RGB Color is selected in the Image > Mode menu, so make sure you have these options selected.

Step 3
Your image should now be completely black and white. Click OK.

Step 4

Now convert the image to grayscale: Image > Mode > Grayscale. A window will appear asking if you would like to discard the color information—click OK. Your image now contains only black and white and is ready to be saved as a JPEG and turned into a vector graphic.

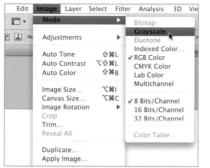

Step 5

However, if your image contains shades, or more than one color, the process is a little different. Once you have opened your image in Photoshop, check that it is in RGB mode and create a black-and-white adjustments layer as before; you'll notice that your image may still contain shades of gray.

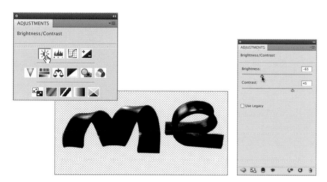

Step 6

Posterizing will make your image purely black and white, but before you do this you may want to adjust the brightness and contrast to control the gray within the image. Through the posterizing process light gray will become white and darker gray will become black, so it's important to adjust the shades first. Go to your Adjustments panel (in the Windows menu) and choose Brightness/Contrast. Play with the sliders until you are happy with the shades of gray.

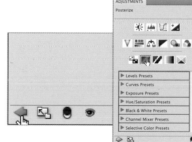

Step 7

Go back to your main Adjustments panel and choose Posterize. Move the slider all the way to the left; you'll see that your image has become black and white only.

Step 8

If you are concerned about the pixelated look of your characters, soften them using the Median function. Go to Filter > Noise > Median and adjust the radius setting until you are happy with the result. Set Image > Mode > Grayscale and save it as a JPEG file. Your image is now ready to be turned into a vector illustration.

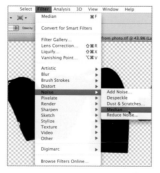

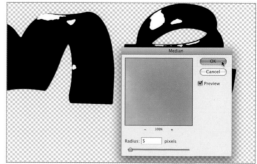

Converting to vector graphics

Each character in your font must be a vector graphic—it can't be a bitmap. The process of converting your characters from bitmaps into vector illustrations can be done in Illustrator. You can also convert colored images into black and white in the same process, if you haven't already done this in Photoshop. Make sure your image is a JPEG file before opening it in Illustrator.

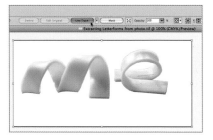

Step 1
The Live Trace feature has lots of adjustable settings. To start with, simply press the Live Trace button in the Control panel (or go to Object > Live Trace > Make).

Step 2
A warning that your object may take a long time to trace may pop up. Unless your image is of an entire alphabet and is huge, you can click OK and deal with this in the settings. If it is of an entire alphabet and huge, consider taking it back into Photoshop and reducing the dpi, before reopening it in Illustrator.

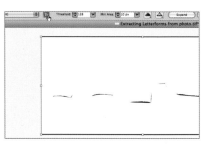

Step 3
Once you click OK, you will see that your image has been traced and, assuming it was color, it will now be black and white. The balance of black and white will probably be incorrect (as above) and you will need to adjust the Live Trace settings. Make sure your image is selected then click the Tracing Options button in the Control panel (Object > Live Trace > Tracing Options).

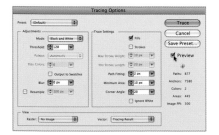

Step 4
When the Tracing Options window appears, check the Preview box. This will allow you to see the effect of any setting adjustments you make.

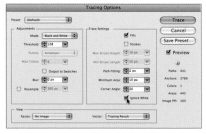

Step 5
Next check the Ignore White box. This means any areas of white in your original characters will not be traced—instead they will be negative space.

Step 6
If you are concerned that your image is very large, now is the time to resample it. Check the Resample box, and reduce the px (pixel) value.

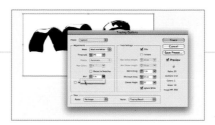

Step 7

Now you need to adjust the black-to-white ratio by moving the threshold slider. Move it to the right and your image will contain more black, to the left and it will contain more white (negative space).

Step 8

If, once you're happy with your black-to-white ratio, you feel that your characters have too much of a pixelated quality, you can soften the lines by applying a blur.

Step 9

When you're satisfied with your adjusted settings, click Trace.

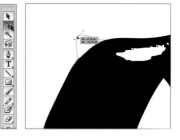

Step 10

The only thing left is to expand your image so that it separates into separate shapes, each with its own vector path. This commits you to the settings you applied in the Trace Options window. To do this simply click the Expand button in the Control panel.

Step 11

The elements of your image will still be grouped together—ungroup them now by going to Object > Ungroup (shift + cmd + g). Each individual element of your orginal image will now be a vector illustration with its own path.

Step 12

Since each element has its own path, you can now adjust those paths if you wish. You can use the Direct Selection Tool to pull the anchor points and adjust their position, or move their handles to adjust the curves of the lines.

Step 13

Or you can use the Delete Anchor Point Tool or the Add Anchor Point Tool to simplify or add to a shape.

Step 14

You may also want to take this opportunity to make sure all your characters are in the correct proportion to each other. Once you're completely happy, save your files, and you're ready to turn them into a font.

Chapter 7:

Creating a font family

Once you know how to prepare your lettering as type, you can move into FontLab or Fontographer to create a working font. On the following pages you will find a step-by-step guide to how this should be done.

Using FontLab and Fontographer

* These notes are written for Mac OS X users with equivalents for Windows XP.

Apple Macintosh and Windows comparison

- ⌘ command (z) on Mac is control on Windows
- ⌥ option on Mac is alt on Windows

- Where key combinations are shown, Mac is given first, with Windows following. In text they are written as, for example, cmd + a (ctrl + a).
- If you are using a single-button mouse on Mac, the right-click function can be performed by using ctrl + click.
- The Preferences dialog on Mac is Options on Windows. To access Preferences, go to FontLab Studio in the Menu bar and scroll down to Preferences. To access Options go to the Tools menu and scroll down to Options.

FontLab and Fontographer Tool palette comparison

The Pen Tool is used for creating straight and curved lines: clicking once, moving, and clicking again produces a straight line; clicking, holding the mouse button down, and dragging produces a curved line with Bézier control points. FontLab also provides a palette that can be used to create several geometric shapes. The principle is similar in Illustrator and Fontographer.

FontLab main Tool palette

Edit Tool: for selecting and dragging objects

Knife: for breaking outlines or inserting nodes

Pen Tool: the main drawing tool

Add Curve Point

Rectangle Tool

Rotate Tool

Slant Tool

Eraser: for deleting (click this over a node to delete it)

Ruler Tool: for measuring parts of the glyph

Add Corner Point

Add Tangent Point

Circle Tool

Scale Tool

Free Transform Tool

Fontographer main Tool palette

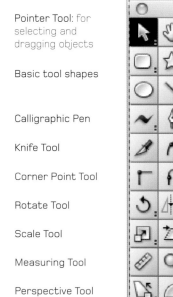 

Pointer Tool: for selecting and dragging objects

Basic tool shapes

Calligraphic Pen

Knife Tool

Corner Point Tool

Rotate Tool

Scale Tool

Measuring Tool

Perspective Tool

Hand Tool: to scroll sceen

Basic tool shapes

Pen Tool

Curve Point Tool

Tangent Point Tool

Flip Tool

Skew Tool

Magnifying Tool

Arc Tool

The following workthrough uses the font Avec, which was born of a collaboration between designers at London-based Praline and The Model Shop at Rogers Stirk Harbour & Partners (RSHP) as part of the If You Could Collaborate exhibition.

ABCDEFGHI JKLMNOPQR STUVWXYZ

Creating a new font

There are three ways to create a new font in FontLab:

1. by clicking on File and scrolling to New;

2. by clicking on the New Font symbol on the tool bar; or

3. by using the keyboard command cmd + n (ctrl + n).

File	Edit	View	Contour
New			⌘ N
Open...			⌘
Open Installed...			O
Search...			
Close			⌘ W
Save			⌘ S
Save As...			⇧ ⌘ S
Save All...			
Revert			⇧ ⌘ R
Generate Font...			⌥ ⌘ G
Generate All...			
Generate Suitcase...			
Import			▶
Export			▶
Font Info...			⌥ ⌘ F
Page Setup...			
Print...			⌘ P

 FontLab Studio   File   Edit   View

New Font (Cmd-N)

In Fontographer
In Fontographer the first two options are the same, but it does not have the tool bar icon.

Using FontLab and Fontographer

The Font window

Each character has its own position or slot. On a New Font window, these slots display with a reference character in gray. The character name is given in the narrow yellow box above each character slot.

The ascent and descent lines define the maximum depth of the character. If a character exceeds these lines there is a danger that it will crash into the next line of text. The cap height defines the vertical limit of straight-line characters such as E, H, M, N, etc. The baseline defines the line on which all straight-line characters sit. Curved characters sit slightly above and below these lines. The x-height line defines the height of lowercase characters.

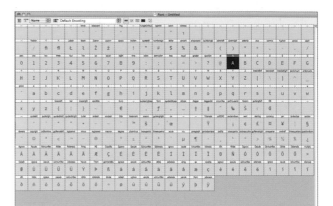

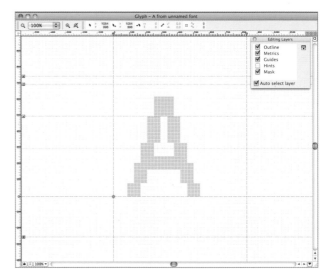

In Fontographer

The Fontographer window is slightly simpler. It doesn't show the maximum ascent line, nor does it have the facility to dock the tool boxes—they remain floating and can be moved anywhere on the screen.

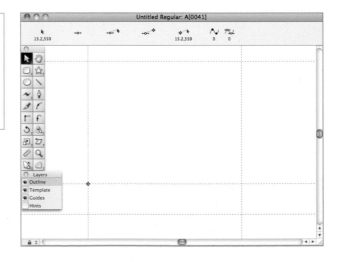

Font Info panel

Use the Font Info panel to set the various parameters that create the identity of the font. The following are the basic fields you need to fill:

➤ Family name: this refers to the main font name—enter your chosen font name here.

➤ Weight: this identifies the weight of the font when there is more than one font with the same name. If you are producing only one font then set the weight as Regular.

➤ Build Names: click on this button to automatically fill in the remaining fields.

The other important dialog box to fill is Font copyright information. The basic fields in this are:

➤ Created by: fill this in with the copyright owner's name.

➤ Creation year: enter the current year.

➤ Build Copyright and Trademark records: click on this to fill in the remaining fields automatically.

In Fontographer

The Font Information panel offers a simpler approach, and has an Easy option. This requires you to enter just the font name in the Family name field, and has drop-down menus for selecting width, weight, slope, etc.

1. Enter the font name. You can also enter the name of the font vendor and designer.
2. Select the font weight from the drop-down menu— Regular if the font has only one weight.
3. Select the font encoding from the drop-down menu.
4. The Advanced mode in Fontographer offers a more comprehensive approach to entering information, but follows the same drop-down menu system.

Using FontLab and Fontographer

Origination

Many type designers prefer to use drawings of their designs rather than start by digitizing directly in the Glyph window: it is easier to judge the character designs when they are placed next to each other and it is also easier to try out different ideas. Once the design has been finalized, the drawings can be scanned and placed in the background layer to use as a guide for digitizing the glyphs. Ideally, the drawing should have a 2in (50mm) cap height. This is large enough to contain good detail of serifs, etc., but small enough to fit several characters on a sheet for scanning. Take as much care over your drawings as possible if you intend to produce classic roman or sans designs.

Importing

Unfortunately there seems to be a glitch when pasting images from Photoshop into FontLab—the images always scale to the cap height even if the image is of a lowercase character. But it is possible to scale the template by double-clicking on the gray template image, grabbing the corner points, and dragging it to size. Hold down the Shift key to ensure the template stays in proportion. To make sure that all the images are in proportion with each other, place guidelines in Photoshop to mark the maximum ascent and descent of the design and then drag a marque around the character using these guidelines before copying and pasting them into an opened FontLab Glyph window.

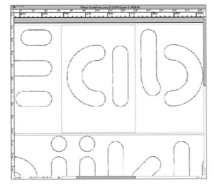

Images can also be imported into FontLab by using File > Import > Background. The images to be imported must all be separate, otherwise they will all be placed in the background layer as a single file. It is best, therefore, to scan each image separately using the same scanner settings each time to ensure a consistent result. Use 1000 pixels high and as wide as required for each character.

It is important to set the scanner to black and white and to save the image as a TIFF. When scanning pencil drawings, scan in grayscale, then adjust the contrast and brightness to obtain a black-and-white image (see pages 152–153 for tutorial). Finally, change the image from grayscale to bitmap and save it as a TIFF.

In Fontographer
Use the same method as with FontLab, but paste into the Template layer. The template images will be in proportion.

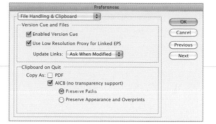

Importing from Illustrator into FontLab

For this stage it is important to have both FontLab and Illustrator open at the same time. Although the drawing tools in FontLab are excellent, you may prefer to use Illustrator for origination. Pasting outlines directly into FontLab from Illustrator will not work with the default settings in Illustrator. Before importing an image it is

important to ensure that the Clipboard settings in Illustrator Preferences are set to Copy As AICB (no transparency support) and also that the Preserve Paths button is checked. If this step is not taken then the image will be imported into the background layer as a gray

bitmap. I also recommend changing the measurement units to Points in the Units & Display Performance box in Illustrator Preferences, as this corresponds to the default measurements used in FontLab.

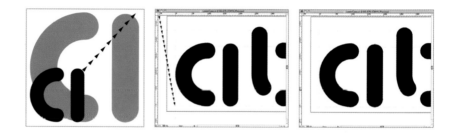

Ensure that Rulers are enabled in the window—cmd + r (ctrl + r)—and then:

1. Scale all of the drawings to 700-point (247mm/9¾in) cap height. Take the measurement from the cap E as this is the standard character to use for cap height.

2. Click in the top left-hand corner of the window at the meeting point of the Rulers and drag the zero point down to the bottom left of the character. Do this for each subsequent character.

3. In Illustrator, select the character and copy it: cmd + c (ctrl + c).

4. Open a character slot in FontLab by double-clicking it.

5. In FontLab, paste [cmd + v (ctrl + v)] into the open Glyph window. The character will be pasted in at the correct cap height and on the baseline.

6. Close that character slot and open the next slot. Repeat this process until all the characters have been copied and pasted into their slots in FontLab.

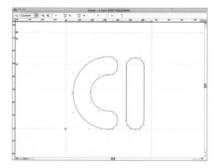

In Fontographer

The procedure is similar, but the images in Illustrator must be prepared in a different way.

1. With the Rectangle Tool in Illustrator, create a square slightly deeper than the ascent and descent of the character.

2. Place this over the first character to be copied, select the character and the rectangle, then copy both [cmd + c (ctrl + c)].
3. Select a character slot by clicking once on it and then paste [cmd + v (ctrl + v)] directly into that slot.
4. Open the character and delete the box; leave just the character.

5. Repeat until all characters have been copied.
6. Because a rectangle has been pasted in with the character, it will appear as a black square in the character window— open the character slot and delete the rectangle.

Using FontLab and Fontographer

Metrics

A very important element in the look of the font is the spacing of the characters. The aim is to produce a visual balance. Ideally each character should appear centered between the characters either side of it.

To begin, open the Metrics window (cmd + opt + shift + m [ctrl + alt + shift + m]) and enter a string of characters. I recommend that you use a combination of straight and curved characters, such as HOHIOOonoioo, as a base from which to establish the side bearings for straight-to-straight, curve-to-curve, and straight-to-curve combinations in caps and lowercase. These values can be then be applied to all of the characters with straight or curved sides. On the right-hand side of the Metrics window is a values box—you can enter the metrics values directly into this.

When spacing the more irregularly shaped characters, such as F, K, V, X, s, v, x, y, z, etc., place them between two straight-sided characters and two curved characters—HVHOVO—and adjust the side bearings until the character looks visually centered. Usually, applying a zero or small minus value (–10) on each side of diagonal characters works as the visual balance can be adjusted by applying kerning.

With FontLab it is possible to import text files into the Metrics window by clicking on the Options button on the right of the text string box.

Don't forget to assign a value to the word space; this is usually between 200 and 300.

It is possible to automatically create side bearings by using the Auto feature.

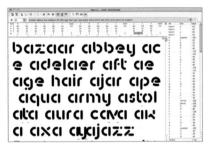

In Fontographer

There are no significant differences in importing from Illustrator into Fontographer. As with FontLab, Fontographer has an Auto feature for creating side bearings.

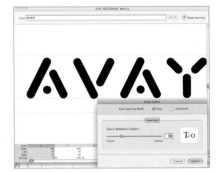

Kerning

To activate the kerning function in FontLab, click on the AV button on the top menu bar in the Metrics window. The vertical side bearing lines will be replaced with a kerning control line placed on the left side bearing. To adjust the kerning, click on the line and drag it to the left to close the gap between it and the character on the left. Kerning can also be controlled by clicking on the box centered underneath the metrics values and entering a minus number, for example −60. To move to the next box, press TAB on the keyboard; to move back press Shift + TAB.

It is also possible to enter kerning values directly into the kerning values column on the right-hand side of the Metrics window. This is useful if certain values are repeated, for example, for Ta, Te, To, Ya, Ye, Yo, etc. You can create kerning automatically by using the Auto feature.

	1st	2nd	Value
	hyphen	A	−60
	hyphen	Y	−60
	hyphen	a	−60
	hyphen	y	−60
	A	question	−100
	A	C	−30
	A	G	−30
	A	O	−45
	A	T	−90

To generate a font file go to File > Generate Font (or the shortcut cmd + opt + g [ctrl + alt + g]).

Select the chosen font format and click Save.

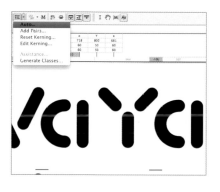

In Fontographer
There are no significant differences in generating a font with Illustrator. Again, Fontographer has an Auto feature for creating kerning.

PROFILE Praline

London, UK

Praline is an award-winning graphic design studio working in art direction and design. Led by creative director David Tanguy, Praline's clients are many and varied. They include the London Design Museum, the Centre Pompidou in Paris, the Tate Modern, Central St. Martins College of Art & Design, and the British Council, as well as the Probeda Gallery, Russia, and Taipei Fine Arts Museum, Taipei. "Our aim when working on projects is to marry the vision of our clients with our own nuanced style," explains Tanguy. "Our work is inspired by all sorts of things ... colors, strange-looking types, clever ideas, beautifully crafted printed work, stories, and architecture. As a design studio we are always discovering something new, whether it's new ways to work or a new subject we don't know anything about." As a company they very much push the boundaries of design, experimenting with different methods, materials, and processes, as can be seen by the work shown here.

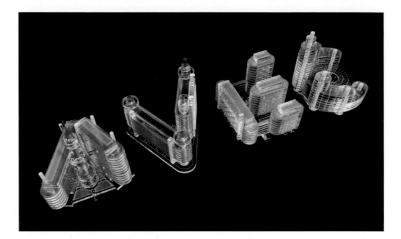

▲ *Illustration*

Avec

Avec is a coming together of Praline's graphic approach and RSHP's expertise in architectural 3D representation. Initial sketches for the type were the result of a complete interaction between model-maker and designer, both sketching on the same piece of paper or in the same notebook, completing each other's ideas. From these initial sketches, four "flat" letterforms were developed using Adobe Illustrator. Then the four Avec models were realized in 3D form, photographed to bring them back to 2D, and then imported into Adobe Photoshop and then Fontlab, where a full working font family was created.

Chicago, USA

Shawn Hazen, now a freelance designer, worked in San Francisco for 10 years for MetaDesign, Chronicle Books, *Dwell* magazine, and Apple. He now specializes in visual design for brands, working largely with small independent companies and start-ups. "I understand the building of brands very well, but I like to focus on what graphic design specifically can do to make a brand special. I love seeing a clever solution, not just design, but something with a smart turn of phrase or visual pun or something that makes you do a double-take." While Hazen always starts his projects with pencil sketches, his process quickly moves to the computer in most cases. "I love the fact that I can make a living making things, creating things, designing things," he adds. "I'd have to do it anyways—it's a compulsion that never lets up—so I feel really lucky to be able to have turned it into something I'm actually supposed to be doing every day."

Theatre and Interpretation Center at Northwestern University presents
WALLIS WORKS-IN-PROGRESS

From the stories of
Nathaniel Hawthorne

Adapted and directed by
Chloe Johnston

February 6–14, 2009
Fri 8pm, Sat 2pm & 8pm, Sun 2pm

Hal and Martha Hyer Wallis Theater
1949 Campus Drive, Evanston

Tickets: (847) 491-7282 or
www.tic.northwestern.edu

General admission $10
Free to 2008/09
Mainstage Subscribers

The 2008/09 Season
is sponsored by

◄ *Poster*
LOOK AND FEEL
The lettering for this promotional piece was created using found ephemera and collage to create the word Look and fake fur to create the word Feel.

▲ *Poster*
TWICE TOLD
The lettering on this poster was created using found twigs. Hazen simply twisted the letterforms into shape and photographed them on a light box.

Hazen often creates typefaces by hand and then digitizes them to turn them into complete working fonts. This type was originally hand-drawn by Hazen using a pencil and notebook. He went through the entire alphabet writing out each letter twice before moving on to create punctuation marks, including an exclamation mark, period, arrows, and the frequently used @ sign. The reason Hazen recommends creating two versions of each letter, even if it is an all-cap type, is because this will allow you to have a variation of each letter, therefore making your final work appear even more "handmade" when it is typeset.

INGREDIENTS

- Scanner
- Adobe Photoshop
- Illustrator
- TypeTool by FontLab

Step 1

Once you have hand-drawn flat letterforms, scan the type and import it into Photoshop. Scan as grayscale and at least 600dpi. Higher resolution is even better, and you could even enlarge it as you scan.

Step 2

For converting your letterforms to a solid black-and-white image, see the tutorial on pages 152–153.

Step 3

For converting your image to a vector graphic, see the tutorial on pages 154–155.

Step 4

With the vector versions of your letterforms created, grab a font that has similar proportions to your new letterforms—condensed, extended, etc.—and open it up in TypeTool. Double-click the capital H, select, and copy it.

Step 5

Now go over to Illustrator and paste the capital H into a new 12 × 12in (30 × 30cm) document. You'll see that it will be very large and almost fills the page. Next, draw some guides around your letter, turn on the rulers with cmd + r or View > Show Rulers, and drag them out from the left and top to denote the sides and top and bottom of your letter.

*TIP

Ensure that you draw the type in black pen, or very dark pencil on white. In order for it to become a font, it needs to be solid black and white, no grays or shading.

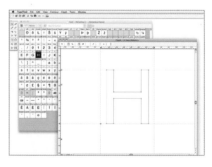

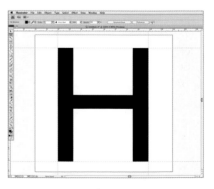

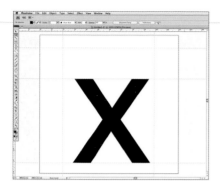 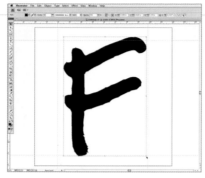 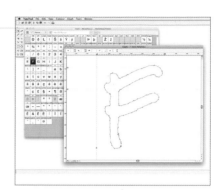

Step 6
If the font you are creating has lowercase, delete the capital H, go back to TypeTool, grab a lowercase x, go back into Illustrator, and paste it in your document. Align its bottom with the bottom guide of the box you created, and drag a horizontal guide to line up along the top edge of the x. You have now created the x-height of your font.

Step 7
Go back to the autotraced Illustrator document that contains the vector version of your letterforms. Copy one of your letters and paste it into your new Illustrator guide document. Size it up according to your guides and then copy it.

Step 8
Go back into TypeTool and double-click the corresponding letter in the font menu to open its window. Paste your letterform in its window. Be sure to note the placement of the existing letter with respect to the dashed lines. Close the Glyph window and hit Save.

Step 9
Again go back to the autotraced Illustrator document with the vector version of your letterforms. Select a new letterform, go back to TypeTool, delete the previous letter, and paste in the new one. Be sure to position in the same place as the previous one and then close the Glyph window and hit Save.

Step 10
Repeat this for all the characters in your alphabet. You can check your progress as you go by using "Quick check as" under the Tools menu.

TIP
The space between the sides of your letter and the vertical dashed lines determines the letterspacing for that character. You may want to drag these lines around a little to adjust it or even it out.

Step 11
Once you've completed all your letters, deleted any existing ones, and renamed the font, go to File > Generate Font. Your font is now ready to use.

TIP
To avoid legal troubles, delete any characters from the existing font that you are not using. Also, open Font Info from the File menu and change the naming and copyright info under the first two options.

PROFILE Corey Holms

Fullerton, USA

Corey Holms is a Chicago-based designer who runs his own home-based studio working on identity and collateral design, as well as designing typefaces both for clients and for his own enjoyment. "The potential of a project is my greatest inspiration," he explains. "Most of my work comes from ideas that have been rejected by others that I think have great promise and that I want to see fulfilled." When creating typefaces Holms tends to "jump right into a project" and then flush out ideas as the work progresses. "I will work with an idea until it doesn't feel right, then I will try out another idea," he explains. "Often, I will come back to an old idea, find something interesting in it, and work on it again. This process sometimes means that the original idea of a typeface can occur years before its completion. Designing is a puzzle and a long process that doesn't always work but when it does it feels really, really good. It's easy to come up with a couple of cool letters, but to create a complete typeface is a constant give and take. You have to keep enough to give it character, but give up enough so that it works with the rest of the pieces."

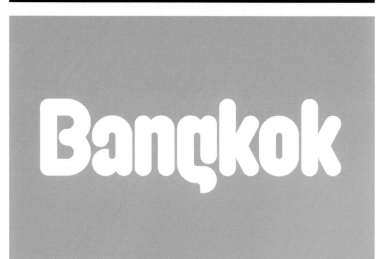

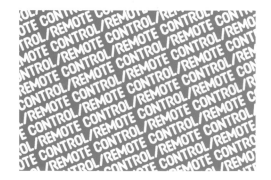

▲ ▶ *Granule font in signs*
THIS PAGE IS TO BE READ LEFT TO RIGHT. / BANGKOK / REMOTE CONTROL
This font was drawn in Illustrator. Holms began with modular shapes, breaking the rules as needed to give these characters the look he was after.

▶ *Ne10 font in use*
NE10: A STENCIL TYPEFACE BASED ON THE GLASS TUBES FROM NEON SIGNS.

Inspired by neon signs, Holms created this font by drawing out the letterforms on graph paper before taking it into Illustrator and drawing the letterforms out as a monoline font. The glyphs were then copied into FontLab so as to create a working font.

Ne10
A stencil typeface based on the glass tubes from neon signs.

▲ *Area font*
Alphabet

Area was inspired by 1970s discotheque culture. "I wanted to refer to the 1970s within the design but equally I wanted to create a font that sat well in today's fashion and club culture," Holm explains. Area originally started life as a few geometric sans serif letters made for a logo. Holms drew the letters in Adobe Illustrator and they were based on the idea of a simple circle. Basing the forms on sans serif makes the entire word become one long ligature. The negative kerning of this typeface means that Holms had to be sure that all the glyphs would work with each other. He did this by testing and fixing the font in FontLab. Because this typeface has multiple ligatures, Holms carried out the OpenType programming in FontLab as well.

Glossary

ascender
The vertical stroke of a lowercase character that rises above the x-height, as with b, d, and h

baseline
The nonvisible line on which letters sit

Bézier points
Named after Pierre Bézier, these are used to describe and control the outline of a glyph

descender
The vertical stroke of a character that falls below the baseline, as with j, p, and y

display type/display lettering
Type or letters that are used at larger sizes for shorter amounts of text, most often for titles and headings

fond
The name under which fonts are organized into font families in Mac OS; this is not used in Windows

font (fount)
The complete character set of a particular typeface in a particular size or style

font family
A group of fonts in a range of point sizes and weights designed to work together, e.g. Arial Black, Arial Bold, Arial Rounded

glyph
A visual representation of a letter, number, or symbol

kerning
The balancing of the white space between two characters, for example in the grouping AWA, to give an even color to the font

letter
A symbol representing a speech sound; a constituent part of an alphabet

letterform
The shape of an individual letter

lettering
Characters built from multiple actions or strokes

lowercase
The small letters of a particular alphabet

metrics
The measurements of the glyph: the width, ascent, and descent

negative space
The space around and within a letterform

OpenType
A universal computer font format designed to enable cross-platform use. It allows more than 65,000 glyphs and thus facilitates multi-lingual and advanced typography

sans serif
A typeface without serifs

serif
A small decorative stroke at the end of a letterform

side bearings
The left-hand and right-hand space assigned to every character

stroke
A single mark (straight or curved line) used to create a letterform

TrueType
An outline font format used mainly on Windows and other PC-based operating systems. TrueType fonts can be used for both screen display and printing

type
Characters designed to be uniformly reproduced through a single action

typeface
A set of one or more fonts of related design in one or more sizes, consisting of a complete alphabet, numerals, and punctuation marks

typography
The art of selecting and arranging type

uppercase
The large or capital letters of a particular alphabet

x-height
The height of the lowercase characters, taken from the lowercase x

Contact details

Daniel Abbott
www.axelburger.com

Airside
airside.co.uk

Amandine Alessandra
www.amandinealessandra.com

Atelier 152
www.a152.nl

BANK
www.bankassociates.de

Raphaël Bastide
www.raphaelbastide.com

André Beato
www.andrebeato.com

Ian Bilbey
www.ianbilbey.com

Fanny Bostrom
www.fannyb.com

Yulia Brodskaya
www.artyulia.com

Erik Buckham
www.palaceworks.com

Andrew Byrom
www.andrewbyrom.com

Cake With Giants
www.cakewithgiants.com

Lisa Congdon
www.lisacongdon.com

Keetra Dean Dixon / FromKeetra
www.fromkeetra.com

Karina Eibatova
www.be.net/eikaDopludo/frame/all

Enormous Champion
www.enormouschampion.com

Christine Föllmer
www.christinafoellmer.de

Jessie Ford
www.jessieford.co.uk

Thomas Forsyth
www.thomasforsyth.com

Jason Grube
www.jasongrube.com

James Gulliver Hancock
www.jamesgulliverhancock.com

Alina Günter
www.alinaguenter.ch

Hand Made Font
www.handmadefont.com

Handverk
www.madebyhandverk.no

Hansje van Halem
www.hansje.net

Sebastian Haslauer
Country: Neath, UK

Adam Hayes
www.mrahayes.co.uk

Shawn Hazen
www.hazencreative.com

Paul Heys / Dtam-TM
info@dtam.co.uk

August Heffner
www.augustheffner.com

Jessica Hische
jessicahische.com

Hjärta Smärta
www.hjartasmarta.se

Cory Holms
www.coreyholms.com

Honey Design
www.honeydesign.com

Troy Hyde
www.troyhyde.co.uk

Inventory Studio
www.inventorystudio.co.uk

Alex Jahn / USE USE
www.useuse.de

Ruiter Janssen
www.ruiterjanssen.nl

Evelin Kasikov
www.evelinkasikov.com

Sarah King (Evening Tweed)
www.sarahaking.com

Vladimir Končar
www.koncar.info

Andrew Lister
www.andrew-lister.co.uk

Charlotte Lord
www.charlottelord.co.uk

James Lunn
www.nnul.co.uk

Me Studio
www.mestudio.info

Natasha Mileshina
www.bubbo-tubbo.com

Milkxhake
www.milkxhake.org

MrYen /
www.mr-yen.com

Jason Munn / The Small Stakes
thesmallstakes.com

Al Murphy
www.al-murphy.com

Ed Nacional
ednacional.com/2009

Mathilde Nivet
www.mathildenivet.com

Mia Notling
www.mianolting.com

Tyrone Ohia
www.tyroneohio.com

Karin von Ompteda
quantitativetype.com

Natsuki Otani
www.natsukiotani.co.uk

Pentagram
www.pentagram.com

Pepper & Cinnamon
www.pepper-cinnamon.net

Plenty
www.Plenty.tv

Praline
www.designbypraline.com

Ben Prescott
www.benjaminprescott.co.uk

Alex Purdy
www.graphdrome.com

Radio Graphics
www.radiographics.jp

Abba Richman
www.abbarichman.com

Lisa Rienermann
www.lisarienermann.com

Rinzen
www.rinzen.com

Alex Robbins
www.alexrobbins.co.uk

Chris Rubino / Studio 18 Hundred
www.studio18hundred.com

Richard Scott
www.richardmalcolmscott.co.uk

Smart Emma
www.smartemma.co.uk

Sneaky Raccoon
www.sneakyraccoon.com

Stay Nice
www.staynice.nl

Alice Stevenson
www.alicestevenson.com

Erik Tabuchi
www.erictabuchi.fr

Daryl Tanghe
www.dtanghe.com

Toben
tottcom.au

Underline
www.underlinestudio.com

Unfolded
unfolded.ch

Alex Varanese
www.alexvaranese.com

Walrus & Eggman
www.walrusandeggman.com

Stuart Whitton
www.stuartwhitton.co.uk

Working Format
www.workingformat.com

J. Zachary Keenan
www.j-zachary.com

Andrea Zeman
www.andreazeman.com

Index